Cyka Blyat!

(or Suka Blyat?)

Everyday Russian Slang and Curse Words

TABLE OF CONTENTS

INTRODUCTION

If you've ever thought about visiting Russia or studying Russian language, culture and people, this book is a MUST have!

I have always wanted to write a book about Russia and its slang for people who are interested in this fascinating topic. So many foreigners have come up to me and asked, "What does Cyka Blyat mean?". Perhaps you found this book while searching for this phrase on the internet. I've been asked this question so many times! One day it hit me, and I decided to write this book and title it "Cyka Blyat! (or Suka blyat?): Everyday Russian Slang and Curse Words."

As you can see from the title, the popular search term "Cyka blyat" is actually a misspelled version of the phrase "Suka blyat". Many foreigners misspell this phrase because, when written in Cyrillic, the word "Сука" (pronounced "Suka") looks exactly like "Cyka". The correct transliteration, or spelling of this word using the Latin alphabet, is "Suka". Later in this book, you will find out what this phrase actually means, so please keep reading!

Who is this book written for?

The information in this book will be useful to you if:

- you are a traveler and about to go to Russia

- you are dating or want to date a Russian

- you are interested in or study the Russian language

- you have a Russian business partner

- you want to communicate with Russians

These are just a few of the different reasons why you might need Russian slang skills.

If you are a Russia-lover, this book will be especially useful for you. If you want to visit Russia or even live there for a while, it's not enough to know just general information about Russia or speak just a few words of Russian.
You need to know some nuances like slang words, where and when local people use slang and the way they use it to communicate with each other. By knowing all these little things, you'll definitely impress your Russian friends.

Let's make something clear. This is NOT going to be a serious research work; there will be no history of slang and curse words or some Wikipedia style information, etc. Here I will introduce you to the world of real Russian language, and teach you popular slang and curse words, different types of them, which of them are REALLY USED by Russians, and when it is appropriate to use them. Let's go!

CHAPTER 1

What is slang and
what does it include?

Slang is an informal way of speaking used among people that live in the same area. Slang may include curse words as well. Everybody knows that cursing is a huge part of every culture! If you don't want to feel out of your element among Russians, you MUST learn Russian curse words! This will allow you to understand others, as well as express yourself more fully. You will be able to communicate with Russians on a more familiar level since you will be expressing yourself the way they naturally would. You need to be careful though. First, you need to learn in which situations using curse words is appropriate. Otherwise, you will get the opposite result.

One interesting thing you should know is that Russian arguably has more curse words than other languages. Russians literally have a curse word for every situation. For example, in English, there might be one single curse word that is used in many situations, but in Russian, there is a unique and exact word for each specific situation.

Slang and cursing play an important role in the language. They contribute to the well-known richness of the Russian language. With such a rich language, it is no surprise that many world-famous writers and poets are from Russia. You might be surprised to find out that even THEY used curse words in their poems and books!

For example, Pushkin, Esenin, Mayakovsky, and many others loved cursing in their works and even THAT sounded poetic. Here is what 18-year-old Pushkin wrote:

Орлов с Истоминой в постели

В убогой наготе лежал.

Не отличился в жарком деле

Непостоянный генерал.

Не думав милого обидеть,

Взяла Лариса микроскоп

И говорит: "Позволь увидеть,

Чем ты меня, мой милый, **ёб**

Orlov with Istomina, in bed

Lied in his miserable nakedness.

The unpracticed general

Did not excel in "hot business"

Without thinking to offend him

Larisa took a microscope and asked him

"I'd like to see, my dear,

what you **fucked me** with"

Yes, I must admit, Russian slang and curse word usage is a special form of art. The Russians like to say "Russian cursing is our heritage, it is immortal".

But, wait! This doesn't mean you should go to Russia and use curse words left and right. I am here to teach you the tricks that will help you become a pro in this art!

Now, in regards to slang words, you should not confuse them with curse words. Slang is just informal language with frequently used and generally inoffensive words. You can use slang words in more situations than curse words.

Now you might be wondering why Russians like to use slang and curse words so much in their speech?

I will explain why.

As far as just ordinary slang words, I think the answer is clear. We all know why people use slang, for example, to make speech more relaxed, fun, and simple. But even then, Russians have way more slang words than other languages do, and we will talk more about that later.

I receive a lot more questions specifically about curse words. One of the most popular questions is why cursing is so popular and frequently used among Russians.

Russians are very emotional people. They believe that cursing makes the conversation "spicy" and helps you to fully express what you want to say. They also think there are some situations in life in which it is impossible to express yourself with normal words. There are just no other words to describe exactly what they want to say, so they use cursing to accurately express their full emotions. Another interesting reason why Russian people curse a lot is... (you will not believe this)...FOR THE LINKAGE OF THE WORDS! YES!

They truly and sincerely believe that cursing helps them to link the words in a sentence, making their speech sound clearer and better. So sometimes (or better said, often) curse words lose their real meaning and are just there to help a person's speech sound better!

Another popular question I get is how often do Russians use slang and curse words. Well... I must say, very often. Walking on the street, you can hear slang and curse words almost everywhere. It could be teenagers or elderly people speaking. Of course, young people use it more often than elderly people, but they all use it.

However, you should also keep in mind, it all depends on the place. For example, at the theater, you will not hear curse words, but slang is very likely.

Russian people are very interesting people; they have the ability to transform from a person who likes swearing and drinking alcohol, into a sophisticated, well-dressed person at the theater. Yes, this is the way Russian people are. I find it charming, in some ways, because Russians have a very deep soul and they put deep meaning EVEN into their curse words and slang.

So guys, especially for you, I decided to ask a few of my friends why and how often they use curse words.

Let's go!

1. Anna, neighbor

    "I use these words quite often because curse words make the conversation more effective and alive"

2. Maxim, friend

    "I use curse words on a daily basis and I believe that people who use curse words are more honest than those who don't."

3. Victor, business partner

    "I do not use these words often, but when I hit myself accidentally and feel pain, I may curse because it makes the pain weaker."

4. Ekaterina, cousin

    "I think cursing really helps you stay calm. Every day you have so many things to deal with and sometimes curse words express your thoughts better than anything, so yes, I use them often."

5. Nikita, friend

    "Well, I've been cursing with my friends since my teenage years. It makes our talks funnier and relaxed, but of course, I do not use them everywhere and with everyone because I understand that they are not appropriate in some places."

6. Polina, friend

    "I don't use curse words and I don't like when people around me use them because I think they are horrible and using them is not cool at all."

So, you can see that 5 out of 6 people from my list USE curse words and they do it quite OFTEN.

I decided not to ask them about slang words because, as opposed to curse words, I am sure that absolutely all people use slang.

Are you LOOKING FORWARD to knowing the exact most popular Russian slang and curse words?

Stay with me and I will guide you through the world of real Russian, and I promise, you will love it!

CHAPTER 2

What slang words NOT to use

Before sharing the most popular slang and curse words with you, I want to teach you some words which can be confusing, and if used in the wrong situation, may accidentally offend a Russian person. You don't want that to happen, do you?

Here is the list of confusing Russian slang and curse words that you should NOT use when communicating with Russians.

1. **Соска** [sOs-ka] - slang word

The literal translation of this word is **"infant pacifier"** (the plastic thing parents put in a baby's mouth to suck on.) When Russians say this word, they mean a pretty or sexy, but superficial woman. This word is never used when they want to compliment a girl, it is only used to describe a woman with frivolous behavior who they want to spend a night with.

Example: Смотри какая **соска** идет!

Meaning: Look at that **"hot/stunning babe"** walking by!

2. **Пиздатый** (male) [piz-dAtiy] **Пиздатая** (female) [piz-dA-taya] - adjective, curse word

This word is used to refer to **"something very good"**, **"amazing"**. Sounds like a good word, right? BUT! Here you must be very careful! You can only use this word with your close friends. For example, you may use this word to "compliment" a close friend's new shirt, if you know each other very well. However, you should NOT say it to a girl you like! If you tell her that she is **"пиздатая"**, then that will probably be the last time you talk to her. You wonder why? Because this word is perversive, obscene, and vulgar.

Example of how NOT to use: Ты мне очень нравишься, ты такая **пиздатая**!

Meaning: I really like you, you are so **amazing**!

Example of how you can use it: Последний фильм с Ди Каприо **пиздатый**!

Meaning: The last movie with De Caprio is **amazing**!

3. **Палить** [pa-lit'] - slang word

This word means **"to look"**, **"to watch"**. Now you might be thinking, what's wrong with that?

So, I must warn you, you can not use this word with just anyone. This word is only allowed between close friends, otherwise, the person you are talking to will just turn around and leave, or, at best, come to the conclusion that you are a rude person with very bad manners.

Example: Чего ты так внимательно на меня **палишь**?

Meaning: Why are you **looking** at me so attentively?

Here I translated the word **"палишь"** as **"looking"** but this is not 100% correct because the word **"looking"** here has a much ruder meaning. In English, it would be like saying **"why the fuck are you staring at me."**

So think twice before using this word to make sure that it is appropriate for the person you are talking to.

Another meaning of the word "**палить**" is "**to reveal something**", "**to tell everybody about something**".

Example: **Не пали** всем как я зарабатываю!

Meaning: **Don't tell** everybody how I make money!

4. **Хуёвый** (male) [hu-yO-vij] **хуевая** (female) [hu-yO-va-ya] - adjective, curse word

This word is used to say that something is "**shitty**", "**awful**", or "**bad**", but in a much ruder way.

Just like the previous words, you should not use this word with someone you don't know very well. If you want to hint to someone that he or she isn't wearing a really nice outfit today, never use "**хуёвый**", otherwise, this person will get mad!

Example: У тебя сегодня такая **хуёвая** прическа!

Meaning: Your hairstyle is so **awful** today!

Example: Это **хуевый** ресторан!

Meaning: This is a **shitty** restaurant!

5. **Тёлка** [tyOl-ka] - slang word

Literally, this word means **"female cow"**. However, this word is popular among male teenagers and some guys because they use it to refer to girls. It's similar to the word "**chick**", but it is very rude and disrespectful! If you call a girl "**тёлка**", she will definitely get offended.

Example: Эй, смотрите какая классная **тёлка**!

Meaning: Hey, look at that cute **chick!**

So please, if you are in Russia and want to flirt with a pretty girl, do NOT use this word!

6. **Не пизди!** [ne peez-di] - curse word

This is a very harsh way of saying **"don't lie"**.

You can NOT use this phrase with someone who isn't a close friend. And even if it is your close friend, you should use it in a humorous way, otherwise, the person will feel offended.

Example: **Не пизди**, что Наташа дала тебе свой телефон!

Meaning: **Don't lie** that Natasha gave you her phone number!

7. **Ебать** [ebAt'] **, ебаться** [e-bAt'-sya] - curse word

Literally, it means **"to have sex"** or to be more exact **"to fuck with someone"**.

This word is strange in some ways. If you want to suggest or ask someone to have sex with you, do not say the word "**ебаться**". It is very rude. Here is an example of how and when you can use this word:

Example: Она такая некрасивая, кто будет с ней **ебаться**?

Meaning: She is so ugly, who would **fuck with** her?

Another example: Я опоздал на работу, босс будет меня **ебать**!

Meaning: I was late for work, my boss is going to **fuck** me!

8. **Рожа** [rO-zha] - slang word

This somewhat derogatory term means **"face"** or **"facial expression"**. When you are joking with your friend, you might say:

"Ну и **рожа** у тебя на этом фото!" which means "What a **face** you have in this picture!" (Look at your face in this picture!)

That would be OK.

BUT!! You'd better NOT say it to someone you don't really know, even as a joke, because then it will sound rude and you'll be seen as a stupid person.

For example, you should NOT say: У тебя очень милая **рожа**!

Meaning: You have a cute **face!**

9. **Пердак** [per-dAk] - slang word

Literally, it means **"ass"**.

This slang word is popular among boys and teenagers. They use it to describe a girl's ass, but usually in situations where she can't hear them because it sounds vulgar and perverse.

If you talk to a nice girl and want to compliment her ass, you should not say this word. She may get offended and in general, it would not sound pleasing.

Example: Чувак, смотри, у Кати такой крутой **пердак**!

Which means: Dude, look, Kate has a cool **ass**!

10. **Напяливать** [na-pYA-livat'] - slang word

The meaning of this word is **"to put on" (a piece of clothing, accessory, etc.),** but in a way that implies that what they are wearing is ugly or ridiculous. It is usually used when a person put something bad on. It is not recommended to use this word if you aren't sure that the other person is not going to get offended. By saying this word, you are laughing at a person's outfit, but what if he/she really likes it?

Example: Что за шляпу ты вообще **напялила** на свою голову?

Meaning: What kind of silly hat did you **put on** your head?

This phrase sounds very mocking, so even your close friend may feel sad after you say it.

11. **Баба** [bA-ba] - slang word

It means a **"female"**, it could be a girl, a woman, etc. It is very close to the word **"тёлка"** we discussed earlier. You should not really use this word around girls. They hate when boys call them this since it sounds rude and vulgar. However, when girls gossip with each other about a girl they do not like, they call her **"баба"** sometimes too.

Example: Слышал, что у Антона новая **баба**?

Meaning: Did you hear that Anton has a new **girlfriend**?

12. **Буфера** [bu-fe-rA] - slang word

The meaning of this word is **"woman's breast"**, **"boobs"**. It is very commonly used among teenagers, especially boys. It is the same kind of word as **"пердак"**, but it means boobs instead of ass. In other words, it is the boob equivalent of "**пердак**".

Boys like using this word for big pretty boobs. But KEEP IN MIND, if you are on a date with a girl you like, do not use this word!

If you want to compliment her body, use the word **"грудь"** [grud'] **"breast"** instead of **"буфера"**. If you say the latter, she will definitely slap your face and leave. Girls believe that men who use words like this, are stupid and have no good manners.

13. **Дрыщ** (male) [drIsh'] - slang word

This is an offensive way to say that someone is **"skinny"**, **"slim"**. Usually, this word is used to mock boys with no muscles and narrow shoulders. If you are joking with your friends, it is absolutely ok to say this, but if you are in a new company and want to say that someone has a slim body, you should never use this word, because it automatically means something bad or unhealthy. It sounds very insulting, especially for Russian men that want to be strong and fit!

Example: Вася, ты такой **дрыщ**!

Meaning: Vasya, you are **so skinny!**

14. **Хахаль** [hA-hal'] - slang word

This is a humorous way of saying **"boyfriend", "lover", "partner"**. It is nothing bad if you are saying it jokingly to a close friend or relative. However, if you say it in a serious way, the person you are talking to may feel uncomfortable.

How you MAY use this word: Опять у Ани новый **хахаль**! Меняет как перчатки!

Meaning: Anna has a new **boyfriend** again! She changes them like gloves!

How you may NOT use it: У тебя отличный **хахаль**, вы красивая пара!

Meaning: You have a great **boyfriend**, you are a nice couple!

So these were just some of the most popular slang and curse words that you should be careful with. Most of them are okay to use, but you need to pay more attention to where and with whom you use them.

CHAPTER 3

Slang and curse words in a close relationship

If you are in a relationship with a Russian or want to date a Russian, don't waste your time and read on!

You should be aware that the popular slang words, which I will teach you in this book, are not suitable to use in all situations. That is why, in this chapter, I am going to show you slang words that are commonly used by couples in different situations.

Dating a Russian woman is a very popular theme these days! It's no wonder why! Russian women are considered to be the most beautiful women on Earth. That aside, lots of foreign women date Russian men as well. So if you are in love with a Russian or you're just planning to meet one, this chapter is for you!

1. **Капать на мозги** [kA-pat' na ma-zgi] - slang phrase

The literal translation of this phrase is **"to drip on one's brain"** which means **"to really bother"** someone to the point of making them angry and annoyed. This phrase is often used by couples, for example, when a girl annoys the hell out of her boyfriend by telling him something over and over again, or a girl gets pissed off when her boyfriend keeps asking her for massages.

Example: Ты мне **капаешь на мозг** уже целый день!

Meaning: You've just been **really bothering** me all day today!

2. **Гнуть свою линию** [gnut' sva-jU li-ni-jU] - slang phrase

The literal translation of the phrase is **"to bend one's own line"** which means to **"stand one's ground"**, **"insist on having one's own way"**, or **"refuse to give in"**. This phrase is frequently used by couples when one person does not want to agree with the other and keeps arguing.

Example: Пожалуйста перестань **гнуть свою линию**!

Meaning: Please stop **being so stubborn**!

3. **Висеть на шее** [vi-sEt' na she-Ye] - slang phrase

The literal translation of this phrase is **"to hang on the neck"** which actually means **"to do nothing but depend on someone"**. Couples use this phrase while arguing when one person does not want to work and just wants to use their partner's money. The phrase is used only to refer to financial dependence.

Example: Когда ты устроишься на работу и перестанешь **висеть на моей шее**?

Meaning: When will you find a job and stop **depending on me financially**?

4. **Зайка** [zAy-ka] - kind of slang, used by all Russians a lot

Actually, this word by itself is not slang, BUT couples turned this word into "relationship slang". The literal translation of this word is **"bunny"** and I know for foreigners it is kind of weird to call your lover a bunny and not something like "baby"...

But the Russians like calling each other **"bunny"** and this word is very popular. Why am I telling you this? Because MOST LIKELY your girl will call you **"зайка"**, or she will want you to call her that. If you do call her **"зайка"**, she will be very happy.

Example: Ты моя маленькая милая **зайка!**

Meaning: You are my little cute **bunny!**

5. **Пудрить мозги** [pU-drit' maz-gi] - slang

No, this phrase is not the same as **"капать на мозги"** which we discussed earlier. Even though the phrases sound and look alike, they have completely different meanings. This one is literally translated as **"to powder brains"** but actually means **"to fool someone"**. This phrase is used when one partner tries to trick the other.

Example: — Дорогой, мое платье не такое дорогое, как ты думаешь.   — **Не пудри мне мозги**!

Meaning: — Darling, my dress is not as expensive as you think. — **Don't try and fool me**!

This slang phrase can be used not only between romantic couples, but in conversations with anyone else as well.

6. **Хватит базарить** [hvA-tit ba-zA-rit'] - slang phrase

This phrase is very popular and is usually (but not always, of course) used by men. It's hard to explain the literal translation, but it basically means something like **"stop talking that much"**. Be careful with this phrase because even in a close relationship it might sound rude. People usually use it when they are arguing or quarreling.

Example: **Хватит базарить** своей подругой по телефону!

Meaning: **Stop talking so much** to your friend on the phone!

7. **Я от тебя кайфую!** [ya ot te-byA kAi-fu-ju] - slang phrase

This is a very positive phrase! The literal meaning of this phrase is **"I am going wild/crazy for you"**. Which means that your partner really likes you. If you are flirting with someone you like, just say "**я от тебя кайфую**" and your lover's heart will melt!

Example: Ты так шикарно пахнешь, **я от тебя кайфую**!

Meaning: You smell amazing, **I am going crazy for you!**

8. **Мне насрать** [mne nas-rAt'] - slang phrase

Well, **"насрать"** means **"to poop"**. However the actual meaning of the phrase "**мне насрать**" is **"I don't give a fuck"**. This phrase is frequently used when a couple is arguing because, compared to a simple **"I don't care"**, it is much more aggressive and rude.

Example: **Мне насрать**, хочешь ты делать или нет!

Meaning: **I don't give a fuck** if you want to do it or not!

9. **Через жопу** [chE-res zhO-pu] - slang phrase

The literal translation is **"through the ass"** which means **"doing something in a backward, cumbersome manner"**. You can use it in a joking way or while arguing. This phrase is extremely popular among couples, especially young ones.

First, I want to show you how to use it when arguing.

Example: Ну почему ты всегда делаешь все **через жопу**?

Meaning: Why do you always do everything **backwards**?

And here is another example, but in a joking way.

Example: — Я опять разбил свою кружку! — Да у тебя всегда все **через жопу!**

Meaning: — I broke my cup again! — Yeah, you always do everything **backwards**!

10. **Хавать** [hA-vat'] **похавать** [pa-hA-vat'] - slang verb

This is a casual way to say **"to eat"**. It is often used by couples, especially by men when they ask their women what there is to eat. Although it has a pretty neutral meaning, not negative or positive, it is only suitable to use this word if you are in a close relationship, otherwise, it may just seem like you are rude and have bad manners.

Example: Милая я дома! Что есть **похавать**?

Meaning: Honey I'm home! What do we have **to eat**?

11. **Достал** (male) [das-tAl] **достала** (female) [das-tAla] - slang verb

The literal translation is **"to get"** but the true meaning is **"to be annoyed by someone"** to the point that you have had enough.

Example: Ты меня **достала** со своей музыкой!

Meaning: You **annoyed** me with your music! (I'm sick and tired of you and your music!)

These were the most commonly used phrases among couples. Of course, there are many more, but if you learn at least these, you'll already be a pro anyway!

The next topic I would love to discuss with you is slang you can use when you are in a group of friends.

This is also a very useful topic because these phrases will help you to not feel left out when you are with your Russian friends.

CHAPTER 4

Slang among a group of friends

In this chapter, we will discuss the most popular slang words used among close friends. Whenever you visit Russia you will find these words very helpful.

1. **Братан** [bra-tAn] - slang word

This is a casual word for **"brother"** like **"bro"**. This is what Russian men call their close friends. Or when they are drunk, they may also call a stranger on the street **"bro"** if they want to ask for a cigarette or something.

Example: **Братан**, можешь дать мне свою машину на выходные?

Meaning: **Bro**, can I borrow your car for the weekend?

2. **Ты гонишь!** [ti gO-nish] - slang phrase

The literal translation of this phrase is **"you are going fast"**, but actually, it has nothing to do with driving or running, at all. The real meaning of this slang phrase is **"you are saying something untrue"**, **"I don't believe you"**, **"you are lying"**.

Example: — Аня теперь моя девушка. — Да **ты гонишь**!

Meaning: — Anna is my girlfriend now. — Yeah right, **you're lying!**

3. **Хрен знает** [hren znA-yet] - slang phrase

The literal translation is **"horseradish knows".** I know this sounds weird since horseradish is a vegetable, but actually, this phrase just means **"I don't know".**

Russian people use this phrase when they don't know something. Of course, it is not suitable to use if you are not with your friends or someone you know well.

Example: **Хрен знает**, что она хочет от меня!

Meaning: **I don't know** what she wants from me!

4. **Бухать** [bu-hAt'] - slang verb

This is a slang term that means **"to drink alcohol".** The whole world knows that Russians love drinking alcohol, especially vodka.

Example: Мы сегодня с друзьями идем в ресторан **бухать**!

Meaning: Today my friends and I are going to the restaurant **to drink alcohol**!

But keep in mind, **"бухать"** is usually used when it is about drinking a LOT, so a more accurate translation is **"to get wasted".**

Dear men, if you ever decide to take a girl on a date and drink a glass of wine, do not use the word **"бухать"** with her.

5. Тупить [tu-pit'] - slang verb

This verb literally translates as **"to be slow at something"** and we do use it when a person does something slow.

Example: **Не тупи**, пошли быстрее!

Meaning: **Don't be slow**, let's go faster!

But there is another meaning of the word **"тупить"** which is **"being dumb"**, **"not getting it"** and we use it this way even more often. Russians use this word on a daily basis, but of course, only with people that they are close with. If you do not know a person well and use this word in the conversation, he/she might get offended.

Example: Я тебе это уже много раз объяснял, **не тупи**!

Meaning: I already explained this to you many times, but you still **don't get it! Don't be dumb.**

Another example: Вот я **туплю**! Это же так просто!

Meaning: Oh, I'm **being dumb**! It's actually so simple!

6. Продинамить [pra-di-nA-mit'] - slang verb

The literal meaning of this word is **"not doing what was promised"** or **"not showing up"**. Russian people like using this verb when talking about each other.

Example: Катя **продинамила** меня и не пошла со мной в клуб.

Meaning: Kate **flaked on me** and didn't go to the nightclub with me.

Another example: Макс обещал помочь, но **продинамил.**

Meaning: Max promised to help, but **didn't do it**.

7. **Туса** [tU-sa] - slang word

There is actually no exact translation of this word in English, but it means **"a party"**. It is frequently used by the younger generation.

Example: Сегодня у Никиты дома будет **туса**!

Meaning: Nikita is throwing **a party** at his place tonight!

There is nothing complicated here, just a simple, easy-to-use word.

8. **Перепихнуться** [pe-ri-pih-nUt'-sya] - slang verb

This is a vulgar way of saying **"to have sex"**, or in other words **"to hook up"**. Mostly used by men, it is not polite to say so to a woman. If you suggest to her to have sex with you by using this word, she will probably say NO to you. You better use this word only when discussing it with your friends.

Example: Я позвал Наташу к себе домой быстро **перепихнуться.**

Meaning: I asked Natasha to go to my place for a quick **hook up.**

9. **Базара нет** [ba-zA-ra nyet] - slang phrase

The literal translation of this phrase is **"no market"**. It doesn't make any sense, does it? Well, actually it means **"no problem"**.

In Russian **"Базар"** means not only a **"market"** but also a **"talk"**. So here, speaking more literally, it means **"no talk"**, **"nothing else to discuss"** meaning **"no problem"**.

You should only use this word with your friends. If someone you do not really know asks you to do something, you can NOT say **"базара нет"**. Otherwise, you will seem impolite and uneducated.

Example: — Скинешь мне эту песню? — **Базара нет.**

Meaning: — Could you send me this song? — **No problem.**

10. **Нажраться** [na-zhrA-t'sya] - slang verb

This word has a very close meaning to the word **"бухать"**, BUT **"бухать"** means drinking alcohol a lot, it's the process, while **"нажраться"** is more like **"being extremely drunk"**, the final result!

Example: Ваня так **нажрался** вчера в клубе, что даже не мог идти.

Meaning: Vanya **got so drunk** yesterday at the nightclub that he could not even walk.

11. **Всеништяк** [vs-yO nish-tyAk] - slang phrase

The meaning of this phrase is **"everything is cool"**. But remember, even though it is not a negative slang phrase, you can not use it when talking with someone you don't know well. This phrase is rarely used by ladies, but frequently by men.

Example : — Как дела? — **Все ништяк!**

Meaning: — How are you? — **Everything is cool!**

The word "**ништяк**" in general means **"cool", "great", "very good"** and you can use it to describe many things and experiences.

Another example: — Тебе понравилась Индийская еда? — Да **ништяк!**

Meaning: — Did you like Indian food? — Yes, it was **great!**

12. **Угарать** [u-ga-rAt'] - slang verb

The literal meaning of this verb is **"to laugh a lot"**. It is a slang word which I recommend you use only with your close friends. It is very similar to **"LMAO"** or **"LOL"** in English.

Example: Я **угараю** с твоих шуток!

Meaning: I'm **laughing so hard** at your jokes!

13. **Лошара** [lo-shA-ra] **лох** [loh] - slang words

The literal translation of these words is **"loser"**. This slang word is used more frequently by men, although ladies use it too. Usually, teenagers call each other "**лошара**" when they are kidding or laughing at each other. It is a quite funny and positive word as long as you only use it with friends.

Example: Ты опять проспал, **лошара**!

Meaning: You overslept again, **loser**!

While teens usually use the word **"лошара"**, everybody else uses the word **"лох"** instead. Here is a funny Russian saying:

Лох это судьба! **Loser** is fate! (Roughly meaning "you were destined to fail/ be a loser, It was your fate to be a loser")

14. **Задрот** [za-drOt] - slang word

We may translate it as **"a nerd"** or **"weird/weak man"**. If a guy doesn't do well in sports or is just simply weak, he will be mocked as a **"задрот"**. Someone who studies a lot, plays computer games, and doesn't go out is also a **"задрот".** Of course, it is a joke word and is usually used by teenagers.

Example: Опять играешь в свои игры весь день? Ну ты **задрот**!

Meaning: Are you sitting at the computer playing games all day again? You're such **a nerd**!

Another example: Владимир не смог подтянуться 10 раз. Он такой **задрот**!

Meaning: Vladimir couldn't do 10 pull-ups. He is **so weak**!

15. **Бабки** [bA-bki] - slang word

This word is used to refer to **"money"** but in a vulgar way. This word is mostly used in casual talks, so you will never hear it from someone speaking in an official manner. In fact, the word **"бабки"** is used a lot by criminals. I recommend you not to use this word because it is not cool at all.

Example: **Бабки** есть?

Meaning: Have you got **money**?

16. **Шляться** [shlyA-t'sya] - slang verb

This verb means **"to hang around"** and is usually used when a person hangs around without a purpose or with bad intentions. It also may be used to talk about frivolous girls. Let me show you a couple examples of how you can use this word.

Example: Ольга всегда **шляется** где попало!

Meaning: Olga always **hangs around** everywhere!

Or here is a phrase every Russian kid has heard from their parents:

Example: Я тебя спрашиваю ты где **шлялся**?

Meaning: I'm asking you where have you been **hanging around?**

17. **Грузить** [gru-zIt'] - slang verb

Literally, it translates as **"to load"**, but in the slang world **"грузить"** means **"to overload someone mentally"** or **"to bore with too much info"**. It is commonly used among Russian youths. You may bravely use this slang verb to express how you feel if someone bores you too much.

Example: Я сегодня очень устал, хватит меня **грузить** разговорами!

Meaning: I am very tired today, stop **overloading** me with your talks!

18. **Чувак** [chu-vAk] - slang verb

Russians like calling their male friends "**чувак**". In English, there is an exact equivalent - "**dude**". BUT keep in mind, "**чувак**" is used only for males!

Example: Эй, **чувак**, позвони мне.

Meaning: Hey, **dude**, call me.

19. **Бомба** [bom-bA] - slang word

Yes, there is an English translation for this word. It is **"a bomb"**. But in this case, it has a little bit different meaning. Here it is meant as a compliment. It may be to a girl, to a car, or even about the weather. But be careful, even though it has a positive meaning, do not say it to a girl you don't really know. She may think you are being vulgar because for a girl it has quite a sexual connotation. Something like **"sexy"**. But keep in mind, hearing this word you should know, the Russians don't mean an actual bomb.

Example: Эта девушка просто **бомба**! Такая **секси**!

Meaning: This woman is **a bomb**! So **sexy**!

Another example: Погода сегодня **чудесная**. Просто **бомба.**

Meaning: The weather is **fantastic** today. Just a **bomb.**

20. Тащиться [ta-shi-t'sya] - slang verb

This verb is translated as **"to drag"** but the slang meaning is **"to be excited about something"** or **"to go crazy for something/someone"**. This word is frequently used by young people.

Example: Этот костюм так тебе идет, я просто **тащусь**!

Meaning: This suit fits you nicely, I just **love it**!

Another example: Я **тащусь** от танцевальной музыки!

Meaning: I'm **going crazy** over dance music!

21. Офигеть [o-fi-gEt'] - slang word

This word is not going to be literally translated because there is no translation for this word. It is a special slang word meaning **"wow!"**

Russians use it when they are pleasantly surprised or happy or when they like something a lot.

Example: Смотрите какая крутая машина, **офигеть**!

Meaning: Look at that gorgeous car, **wow**!

Also, sometimes this word is used to express your emotions better. Let me show you.

Example: **Офигеть**, какой ты крутой парень!

Meaning: **Wow**, you are such a cool guy!

Next time you are in Russia and hear this word, know it is something cool and positive!

So there was just a little portion of the slang words that Russians like to use on a daily basis. I tried to select the most used ones to make your "Russian" life easier.

It is not the end of our journey. I still have so many words and phrases to share with you guys.

So let's not delay and let's go further!

CHAPTER 5

Nightclub Slang

You've probably heard that Russians like partying and nightlife, and it's true. There are lots of night clubs in Russia, especially in Moscow. And if you, my dear Russian travelers and lovers, come to Russia, you must check these clubs out. For that, you need to know the local party slang. Don't worry, that is what this chapter is for. Stay with me!

1. **Отрываться** [at-tri-vAt-sya] - slang verb

The literal translation of this word is **"to come off"** but what we mean here is **"to party hard"** or **"to have a blast"**.

This word is frequently used by people of all ages who like to party.

Example: Вчера мы ходили в клуб и **оторвались** там по полной!

Meaning: Yesterday we went to the night club and **had a blast**!

2. **Нарываться** [na-ri-vAt-sya] - slang verb

The literal translation of this verb is **"to run into"**, but in Russian, this word has a more exact meaning **"to run into trouble"** or **"to look for trouble"**. This word can be useful at the club, for example, if you get into an argument.

Let me show you some examples of how to use it in a real-life conversation.

Example: Парень, ты **нарываешься**? Давай выйдем поговорим!

Meaning: Hey man, are you **looking for trouble**? Let's go outside for a talk!

Another example: Я ехал 120 км/ч и **нарвался** на полицию!

Meaning: I was driving 120 km/hr and **ran into** the police!

3. **Развезло** [ras-vez-lO] - slang verb

There is no exact translation for this slang verb, but it is used to say that someone **"got very drunk"**. Russians drink alcohol quite often and they like using this word when joking about their friends who get drunk fast or have low alcohol tolerance.

Example: Олег, тебе хватит пить на сегодня, тебя уже **развезло**!

Meaning: Oleg, you've had enough to drink for tonight, you are already **drunk**!

4. **Пальцы веером** [pAl'-zy vE-ye-rom] - slang phrase

Literally, this phrase says **"fingers like a fan"**. Actually, it is a gesture when the little and the pointing finger are put forward, and the remaining fingers are pressed to the palm. Like the Illuminati hand sign, you know? In Russia, this gesture comes from the criminal world.

Nowadays, this phrase is used when we want to describe someone that shows off too much. In expensive night clubs, you can easily meet people who show off a lot.

Example: У этого парня **пальцы веером**, просто потому что у него дорогая машина.

Meaning: This guy **is showing off**, just because he has an expensive car.

5. **Обдолбанный** [ab-dOl-ba-niy] - slang word

The literal translation of this word is **"hollowed"** but Russians use it to say that someone is **"drugged"**, **"intoxicated"** or **"high"**.

Example: Иван такой **обдолбанный**! Он наверняка на кокаине!

Meaning: Ivan is **so high**! He must be on cocaine!

6. **Лажовый** [la-zhO-viy] - slang adjective

This slang word means **"poor-quality"**, **"bad"**, **"crappy"**. You should only use this word with friends.

Example: Где ты взял такой **лажовый** телефон?

Meaning: Where did you get such a **crappy** phone?

Another example: Певица спела **лажово**! [la-zhO-vo]

Meaning: The singer sang **very badly**!

7. **Прикольно** [pri-kOl'-no] - slang verb

This slang word is used often by young people, at night clubs, and in many other situations as well. It means **"fun", "cool"**.

Example: Эта девчонка такая **прикольная**!

Meaning: This girl is so **cool!**

Another example: Здесь так **прикольно!**

Meaning: It is so **fun** here!

8. **Тачка** [tA-chka] - slang verb

This word is at the top of the list of most popular Russian slang words. It is used everywhere, but mention it here since it is frequently used at clubs. Funny fact, the literal translation is a **"wheelbarrow"**, but Russians usually mean **"a car"**.

Example: Смотрите на какой **тачке** он приехал.

Meaning: Look at the **car** he arrived in.

Another example: Чувак, зацени какую **тачку** я купил!

Meaning: Dude, check out the **car** I bought!

9. **Крутяк** [kru-tyAk] **круто** [krU-to] - slang word

This word means **"cool", "awesome", "dope"**. It has no literal translation in English, but you can use it in the company of your friends.

Example: — Сегодня мы едем на вечеринку. — **Крутяк**!

Meaning: — Today we are going to a party. — **Awesome**!

Another example: Дорогая, ты так **круто** выглядишь!

Meaning: Dear, you look **dope**!

10. **Разборки** [ra-zbOr-ki] - slang word

Literally, it means **"a conflict situation"**. You know how when you go to the club there is always a bunch of drunk people fighting nearby? This is what we call "**разборки**".

Example: Ты видела какие **разборки** были у Вани и Саши?

Meaning: Did you see the **conflict** between Sasha and Vanya?

11. **Лохануться** [la-ha-nU-tsa] slang verb

This verb has no literal translation, but it means **"to fail"**, **"to make a mistake"**. Russians use this word daily in all sorts of situations, not just at night clubs, but it's definitely a useful word for this topic.

Example: Ты так **лоханулась** вчера когда напилась.

Meaning: You **made a mistake** yesterday when you got so drunk.

Another example: Я хотел познакомиться с девушкой, но **лоханулся**!

Meaning: I wanted to meet a girl, but **failed completely!**

12. **Нарик** [nA-rik] - slang word

I must warn you, this is a super slang word and you can not use it with everyone. **"Нарик"** is a short form of the word **"наркоман"** which is not a slang word and means **"a drug-addict"**. **"Нарик"** is a slang form like **"junkie"**.

Example: Этот Игорь такой **нарик!**

Meaning: Igor is such a **junkie!**

13. **Понтоваться** [pan-ta-vAt-sya] - slang verb

This slang word is translated as **"to show off"** but a bit stronger. For the clubs, it is a very useful word since there are lots of people who go to night clubs to show off.

Example: Он пришел сюда **попонтоваться** своей новой девушкой?

Meaning: Did he come here **to show off** his new girlfriend?

Another example: Зайка ну хватит **понтоваться** своей машиной!

Meaning: Baby, please stop **showing off** your car.

14. **Кипишить** [ki-pi-shit] - slang verb

This word can be translated as **"to fuss"** and is used when someone gets worked up or worried about something for no reason. Even though it has a neutral meaning, use it strictly in the company of your friends. It is a slang word, after all.

Example: Успокойся, **не кипишуй**, пожалуйста!

Meaning: Calm down and **don't fuss**, please!

15. Тусовка [tu-sOf-ka] - slang word

We discussed the shorter version of this word, **"туса"**, earlier. The word **"тусовка"** has the exact same meaning, **"a party"**. It is a frequently used word among Russians, especially the younger generation.

Example: **Тусовка** оказалась классной!

Meaning: **The party** turned out to be great!

16. Зачетная [za-chyOt-naya] - slang adjective

The literal translation of this word is **"tested"**, but Russian people use it as an adjective to describe something or someone, and this adjective has a positive meaning only. In other words, it is something that "passed the test" and they approve of. At nightclubs, there are a lot of girls that are being **"tested"** by the boys' eyes. Simply it has the same meaning as **"great"**, **"cool"**, **"nice"**.

Example: Видел какая **зачетная** девчонка? Пойду познакомлюсь с ней.

Meaning: Did you see that **cool** girl? I'm going to go meet her.

17. Намутить [na-mu-tit'] - slang verb

The closest literal translation of this slang word in English is **"to mix"**, but the actual meaning is **"to get"**, **"to acquire"**. This word is used quite often in nightclubs. Here is an example.

Example: **Намути** мне коктейль, чувак!

Meaning: **Get me** a cocktail, dude!

Keep in mind that you can use this word for pretty much anything, not just drinks or liquid.

Another example: Борис можешь **намутить** билеты на концерт?

Meaning: Boris, can you **find/get** concert tickets?

18. **Подкатить** [pot-ka-tIt'] - slang verb

The literal translation of this word is **"to roll up"**. It actually means **"to become acquainted"**, **"to meet"** with a girl or a boy. But this word implies that it is in a more flirtatious and kind of vulgar way.

Example: Тебе пора бы уже **подкатить** к Свете!

Meaning: It's time for you **to meet** Sveta!

19. **Тухляк** [tuh-lyAk] - slang word

This word comes from the adjective **"тухлый"** which translates as **"rotten".** But in most cases, the actual meaning is **"very boring"**. Russians use this word when they go to a nightclub and it is no fun there, or there are not a lot of people, etc.

Example: Пойдемте в другой клуб, в этом сегодня полный **тухляк**!

Meaning: Let's go to another club, this one is **so boring** today!

20. **Голяк** [ga-lyAk] - slang word

This word sounds similar to the previous one, but the meaning is different. The word **"голяк"** comes from the adjective **"голый"** which translates as **"naked"**. However, when Russians say it, they mean **"empty"**, **"nothing at all"**. Let me show you a few examples.

Example: Брат, можешь заплатить за меня сегодня, у меня по деньгам **голяк**.

Meaning: Bro, could you pay for me tonight please, I **don't have** any money **at all.** (or if being more literal - my money is **naked**).

Another example: В этом магазине нет нормальных продуктов, там всегда **голяк**.

Meaning: There are no good products at that store, it's always **empty**.

21. **Попадос** [pa-pa-dOs] - slang verb

You will not find an English version of this word. It is used to describe an unpleasant situation or a situation where you got into trouble. It is something like **"a fail"**, **"a problem"**, but it sounds more rough and casual.

Example: Она узнала, что я изменяю, это полный **попадос!**

Meaning: She found out that I'm cheating on her, this is a real **problem!**

22. **Зажигать** [za-zhi-gAt'] - slang verb

The literal translation of this verb is **"to light up"** but in our case, Russian people mean **"to have real fun"** or **"to have a blast"**.

Example: Ты сегодня просто **зажег** в клубе!

Meaning: You just **had a blast** at the club tonight!

23. **Взорвать танцпол** [vza-rvAt' tanc-pOl] - slang phrase

This phrase translates to English as **"to blow the dance floor up"**, but it means **"to get everyone to dance on the dance floor"**. Wanna blow up the dance floor when you come to Russia?

Example: Этот новый диджей просто супер, он **взорвал танцпол!**

Meaning: That new DJ is awesome, he **made everybody dance**!

24. **Закадрить** [za-ka-drit'] - slang verb

The closest translation for this word in English would be **"to pick up"**(chicks at the club) or **"to make someone like you"**. To help you understand how to use this word, I want you to imagine a situation: A guy at a nightclub likes a girl very much and wants her to come home with him. She is not sure if she is going to do it, but he does everything to convince her by flirting and giving her compliments. He gets her to like him and then she goes away with him.

Example: — Как так Аня ушла с Максимом? — Да он **закадрил** ее!

Meaning: — How did Anna end up going home with Maxim? — He **picked** her **up**!

25. **Сушняк** [sush-nyAk] - slang word

Most of the time the meaning of this word is **"a hangover"**. **"Сушняк"** literally translates as **"a thirst"**, like when you need to have a drink after a long hard party. A familiar situation for all of us, isn't it?

Example: Я сегодня никуда не пойду, у меня жесткий **сушняк**.

Meaning: I am not going anywhere tonight, I have a strong **hangover.**

Another meaning: Я так долго бежал, у меня большой **сушняк**!

Meaning: I ran for so long, I have a big **thirst**! (I am so thirsty!)

26. Шалава [sha-lA-va], потаскуха [pa-tas-kUha] - slang words

Be careful with these words because they are insulting and extremely rude. The literal meaning of these words are **"whores", "sluts"**. These are suitable words for our club topic because there are lots of sluts at night clubs. So just for your information, you should know this word. Also, some men like using this word to insult a woman even if she is not a slut at all in real life, usually when a couple fights and a man wants to say something mean to his woman, but you should never do it!

Example: Эта девчонка такая **шалава**, она всегда окружена парнями!

Meaning: This girl is such a **slut**, she's always surrounded by guys!

CHAPTER 6

Student life slang

Another popular topic to discuss is studying! Millions of students and pupils use their special "study" slang on a daily basis, and it is definitely something that you should know. What if you end up going to a Russian school or university?

1. **Препод** [prE-pat] - slang verb

This is a shortened form of the word **"преподаватель"** which means **"a professor"**. This is what students in Russian universities call their teachers. However, you should be aware that while in English a single word "teacher" can be used to refer to all teachers, in schools and universities alike, in Russian that is not the case. A teacher in a school is called **"учитель"**, while a teacher at a university is called **"преподаватель"**.

For example: **Препод** сегодня не пришел на занятие.

Meaning: **The professor** didn't show up for class today.

2. **Общага** [ap-shyA-ga] - slang word

This is also a short form of the word **"общежитие"**, which means **"dormitory"**. In English, the word **"dorm"** is used in absolutely the same way as **"общага"**. Yeah, students like shortening words.

Example: Я живу в **общаге**.

Meaning: I live in a **dorm**.

3. Автомат [af-ta-mAt] - slang word

No, this is not a weapon. It is just another popular word related to education and studying. Russian students LOVE this word. Let me explain why.

Teachers use the incentive of an **"автомат"** to encourage students to study very well during the semester. If you get an **"автомат"**, it means you did so well during the semester that you don't have to take your final exams and you get an excellent grade **AUTOMATICALLY**. Yes, this is why they call it "an automatic"!

Example: Кате везет, она получила **автомат**!

Meaning: Kate is lucky, she got an "**exemption from exams**"!

4.Окно [ak-nO] - slang word

This is another favorite word among Russian students. The literal translation of the word is **"a window"** but the actual meaning is **"a slot of spare time between classes"**.

Example: У нас сейчас **окно**, пойдем перекусим?

Meaning: We have **a break** now, let's go have a snack.

5. Зачётка [za-chiOt-ka] - slang word

This is a short form of the phrase **"зачетная книжка"**. The literal translation of this phrase is **"a student's record-book"** but the Russians call it **"зачётка"** for short. I'm guessing you all know what this book is for, but just in case you don't, I'll explain. In Russia, it is a small book with all a student's grades and records, including the exams and tests that he or she has passed.

Example: Смирнов, у тебя отличная оценка, давай **зачетку.**

Meaning: Smirnov, you got an excellent mark, give me your **student record book**.

This phrase is what all Russian students dream to hear!

6. **Прогуливать** [pra-gU-li-vat'] - slang verb

The literal translation of this word is **"to walk around"** but what Russians actually mean when they use this word is **"to skip classes"**. This word is suitable for both university and school.

Example: Если ты не перестанешь **прогуливать** занятия, тебя отчислят.

Meaning: If you do not stop **skipping** classes, you will be expelled.

7. **Вылететь** [vi-le-tet'] - slang verb

The literal translation of this slang word is **"to fly out"** but in our case, it means **"to be expelled"**. Teachers like using this word to scare students.

Example: Ты **вылетишь** из универа если не будешь стараться.

Meaning: You'll be **expelled** from the university if you do not work hard.

8. Шпора [shpO-ra] - slang word

The literal translation of this word is **"a spur"**. However, in Russian slang, it means **"a cheat sheet"** which you bring with you to help you pass your exams. Of course, you have to hide it. **"Шпора"** is a short version of the word **"шпаргалка"** which means **"a cheat sheet"**.

Example: Я написала много **шпор** [plural], надеюсь сегодня они помогут мне сдать экзамен!

Meaning: I made lots of **cheat sheets**, I hope they will help me get a good grade on my exam today!

9. Скатать [ska-tAt'] - slang verb

The translation of this word is **"to roll up"**. However, it is slang for **"to copy"** or **"to cheat on exams"**. If you want to study at a Russian university, you MUST know this word!

Example: Я хорошо сдала экзамен, я все **скатала**!

Meaning: I got a good grade on my exam, I **cheated**!

10. Хвост [hvost] - slang word

The literal translation of this word is **"a tail"** but in the Russian study world, it means **"an obligation"**, a failed exam, or a test that a student still has **"an obligation"** to pass.

Yeah, Russian students do not like this word at all...

Example: У Ольги столько **хвостов**, наверное ее отчислят скоро.

Meaning: Olga has so many **failed exams**, I guess she will be expelled soon.

11. Допка [dOp-ka] - slang word

This is a short form of the adjective **"дополнительная"**. Here it is used to mean **"дополнительная экзаминационная неделя"** which means **"additional examination week"**. This is when a student who failed his exams gets another chance to retake them. But you better get ready for your exams to not fail!

Example: Я буду сдавать **допку**, потому что я завалил экзамен по математике.

Meaning: I will have to **retake a test during the additional examination week** because I failed a math exam.

12. Домашка [da-mA-shka] - slang word

This is a short casual way to say **"домашнее задание"** which is **"homework"**. And yeah, Russian students like this simple version of the phrase. Obviously, the teacher does not use this word, only students do.

Example: Я не сделала **домашку** сегодня.

Meaning: I have not done **homework** today.

13. Липовый [li-pa-viy] - slang adjective

There is a Russian word **"липа"** which means **"linden tree"**, but in this case, we do not mean trees at all. Here, **"липовый"** means **"fake"**, **"phony"**.

Example: Зачем ты дала мне **липовый** номер? Мне нужен был твой.

Meaning: Why did you give me **a fake** number? I needed yours.

14. **Ботан** [ba-tAn] - slang words

The literal translation of this word is **"a nerd"**. This is what Russians call people who do nothing else but study.

Example: Он такой **ботан**, наверное он только и делает, что учится целыми днями.

Meaning: He is such **a nerd**, I think all he does is study all day long.

15. **Тупой** [tu-pOy] - slang adjective

Literally, the translation of this word is **"flat"**, **"dull"**, and the actual meaning is **"stupid"**, **"dumb"**. This is what Russians call people that are not smart. But you'd better not say it to anyone when you visit Russia, since it is quite rude and offensive.

Example: Я не понимаю как он здесь учится, он же такой **тупой**!

Meaning: I do not understand how he manages to study here, he is so **dumb**!

16. **Грузить** [gru-zIt'], **загружать** [za-gru-zhAt'] - slang verb

Literally, it means **"to load"**, but in the slang world **"грузить"** means **"to overload someone with information"** or **"to bother with something"**. It is commonly used among Russian students and pupils when they are given lots of homework.

Example: Я сегодня очень устал, учителя нас просто **загрузили** домашним заданием!

Meaning: I am very tired today, the teacher just **overloaded** us with lots of homework!

Another example: Милая, пожалуйста хватит **грузить** меня своими вопросами!

Meaning: Darling, please stop **bothering** me with your questions!

17. **Спалиться** [spa-li-t'sya] - slang verb

The literal translation of this word is **"to get burnt"** but here it means **"to get caught"**. This is an important word for Russian students when it comes to passing exams!

Example: Я сегодня **спалилась** на экзамене когда списывала.

Meaning: I **got caught** during the exam today while I was cheating.

18. **В шоколаде** [v shi-ka-lA-de] - slang phrase

The literal translation of this word is **"in chocolate"**, but when Russians say it, they mean **"everything is good"**,

"to be in a good place", "to be happy". This slang phrase is used in many different situations, but among students, it is used a lot!

Example: Сейчас я сдам экзамен и все будет **в шоколаде!**

Meaning: Now I will pass my exams and everything **will be great!**

Another example: Когда я заработаю много денег, то буду **в шоколаде**!

Meaning: When I earn lots of money, I'll **be happy**!

19. **Повестись на что-то** [pa-ves'-tls' na chto-ta] - slang phrase

There is no exact translation for this word, but it means **"to believe in something".** Most of the time, it is used when you believe in something and later you realize you've been lied to or scammed. Yes, Russian students are young and naive and they make mistakes that eventually lead to them getting tricked.

Example: Он обманул меня, как я мог **повестить** на это?

Meaning: He lied to me, how could I have **believed** in that?

Another example: Она сказала ему, что не изменяла и он **повелся**.

Meaning: She told him that she never cheated on him and he **believed**.

20. **Запаренный** [za-pA-re-niy] - slang adjective

The correct translation of this word is **"steamed"** but the Russian slang meaning is **"tired", "exhausted", "very busy"**. This is a very useful word for Russian students because they really get tired of studying. You know the Russian education system is not easy at all.

Example: Я уже **запарился** с этим проектом!

Meaning: I am **tired** of this project!

Another example: У меня столько всего происходит, я такой **запаренный**!

Meaning: I have so much going on, I'm **so busy**!

21. **Кипит мозг** [ki-pIt mozg] - slang phrase

This phrase is very frequently used by Russians. If we translate it literally, it means **"the brain is boiling"** but when Russians say it, they just mean that they are **"very tired and puzzled"**.

For example: У меня **кипят мозги** каждый раз после экзаменов.

Meaning: My **brain is** always **so tired**, after finishing exams.

22. **Достать** [das-tAt'] - slang verb

The literal translation is **"to get"** but actually it means **"to wear out"**. This is usually used when you are sick of doing something and want to get rid of it.

Example: Меня **достала** уже эта учеба!

Meaning: The studying has **worn** me **out**!

Another example: Препод **достал** меня! Задает мне вопросы на каждом уроке!

Meaning: The teacher has me **worn out**! He asks me questions in every class!

23. **Зашуганный** [za-shU-ga-niy] - slang adjective

The direct translation for this word is just **"frightened"** but Russian people say it, they mean **"a person who is afraid of everything"**. Why did I choose this word for our study topic? Because you will meet all kinds of people in your classes. Most likely, you will hear this word quite often.

Example: Этот первокурсник такой зашуганный.

Meaning: This freshman is so **afraid of everything**.

24. **Кидалово** [ki-dA-la-va] - slang word

There is no exact translation for this word, but Russians use it often, and it means **"a lie"**, **"a scam"**. This slang word is used in all spheres of life, including studying.

Example: Не верь этому, это сплошное **кидалово**.

Meaning: Do not believe it, it is all a **scam**.

Another example: Будь осторожен с Васей, он всех **кидает**.

Meaning: Be careful with Vasya, he **lies** to everybody.

25. **Крыша едет** [kri-sha E-det] - slang phrase

Literally, the translation is **"the roof is coming off"** but it means **"going crazy"**. Yep, I know it's funny, and it could not be more suitable for our study topic!

Example: Я так устал читать книгу, что у меня **крыша едет**!

Meaning: I am so tired of reading this book, that I'm **going crazy**!

26. **Отмазка** [at-mAs-ka] - slang word

This is a slang word for **"an excuse"**. Russians use it everywhere on a daily basis!

Example: Я не пойду сегодня в универ, найду какую нибудь **отмазку**.

Meaning: I am not going to the university today, I will find **an excuse**.

Another example: Маша хватит **отмазываться**! Пошли на свидание!

Meaning: Masha enough **finding excuses**! Let's go on a date!

Of course, there are many more slang words that can be used in the context of studying and school, but I tried to show you the favorite slang words of Russian students. I hope this information was useful to you!

Another topic I want to share with you is TEENAGE slang. But please, do not confuse this topic with the topic of slang used by young adults. There is a big difference between them, trust me.

CHAPTER 7

Teenagers Slang

In general, young people use just the most popular slang words, which we have discussed with you already (nightclubs, study, relationship, friends), in their everyday life. But teenage slang is a bit different, it is only used by teens between the age of 10 and 17 years old.

What if you marry a Russian woman, stay in Russia, and then have a Russian speaking child? Then you will HAVE to know teenage language to be aware of your child's life.

1. **Авка** [Af-ka] - slang word

This is a short version of the word **"аватар"** which means **"avatar"** or **"profile picture"** which is of course, very popular since teenagers like social media websites and they post lots of pictures of themselves.

Example: Ты видел новую **авку** у Аньки?

Meaning: Have you seen Anna's new **profile picture**?

2. **Бомбить** [bam-bit'] - slang verb

The literal translation of this verb is **"to bomb"**, but actually the meaning has nothing to do with war. We use it to describe the following: **"to be annoyed"**, **"to be** angry", "to shout", "to be nervous". Teenagers use this word a lot while speaking to each other.

Example: Катя рассталась со своим парнем, он всегда на нее **бомбил**.

Meaning: Kate broke up with her boyfriend, he always **shouted** at her.

Another example: Катя меня обманула и не пришла. Меня так **бомбит**!

Meaning: Kate lied to me and didn't show up. I'm so **angry**!

3. **Варик** [vA-rik] - slang verb

This is a shorter form of the word **"вариант"** which is translated as the similar-sounding word **"variant"** or **"an option"**. Russian teens use the short form in their conversations.

Example: Нам вообще не **варик** идти туда сегодня.

Meaning: It is not **an option** to go there today.

4. **Жиза** [zhI-za] - slang word

Oh, how Russian teenagers like this word! They use it literally every day! **"Жиза"** is a short form of the word **"жизненно"**, which is translated literally as **"vital"**. However, the actual meaning is **"true story"**, **"a real-life situation"**. Teens like using this word when they send memes to each other.

Example: — Ты видел мем, который я тебе отправил? — Да, вообще **жиза**!

Meaning: —Did you see the meme I sent you? —Yes, it's so **true**! (I can totally relate to the situation in the meme)

5. **Зашквар** [zash-kvAr] - slang word

There is no translation for this word, but it means **"a shame", "something that is not right", "not cool"**.

Example: Эта музыка уже давно не модная, просто полный **зашквар**.

Meaning: This music stopped being popular a long time ago, it's totally **not cool**.

Another example: Ты знаешь, что Оля изменила своему парню? Это такой **зашквар**!

Meaning: Did you know that Olya cheated on her boyfriend? That is **so not right**!

6. **Паль** [pal'] - slang word

A short form of the word **"палённый"**, meaning **"singed"**, Russian teens use this word to mean **"fake"**. Most of the time, they use it to talk about clothing or other pirated items.

Example: У нее не настоящая сумка Шанель, а **паль**!

Meaning: Her bag is not a real Chanel, it is a **fake**!

7. **Хз** [hэ-zэ] - slang phrase

This is an abbreviation for the phrase **"horseradish knows"** which means **"хрен знает"**. This means **"I don't know", "who knows", "nobody knows"**.

Example: — Ты сегодня пойдешь гулять? — **Хз**

Meaning: — Are you going out tonight? — **I don't know**.

8. **Сасный** [sAs-niy] - slang adjective

There is no translation for this word in English, but teenagers love using it to describe someone who is **"sexy"**, **"nice looking"**, **"beautiful"**.

Example: Настя такая **сасная** девчонка, я о ней мечтаю.

Meaning: Nastya is such a **sexy** girl, I dream of her.

So, these were just a few of the most popular slang words used by Russian teenagers. If you ever get a Russian kid, you will be prepared with the help of my list.

CHAPTER 8

Russian curse words

Guys, this chapter is going to be about Russian curse words. Please, don't confuse curse words with slang words. Slang is a quite harmless language, but I can not say the same about curse words, so be careful!

Russian people LOVE using curse words in their everyday life and there are so many variations of each curse word. Almost all of them can be used both in a comic form and in an evil form. One more thing that I want you to notice is that curse words seldom have an exact translation in English. Cursing in Russian is like a whole other unique language that is truly Russian. Of course, I will explain what every word actually means!

So here I am going to fill you in on this world.

Let's start.

1. **Сука** [sU-ka] - curse word

There is an exact translation of this word in English, it is **"a bitch"**. I guess you all know where and how to use this word.

Example: Она такая **сука**, всегда ведет себя высокомерно!

Meaning: She is such **a bitch**, she always acts arrogant!

2. **Блять** [blyAt'] - curse word

I think this word is going to be at the top of any list of Russian curse words because this is literally the most used curse word.

It is like saying **"fuck", "shit", "damn it"** but with more emotion. It is used everywhere.

P.S. Do not forget that it is a curse word, after all, so don't actually use it everywhere!

Example: **Блять**, я забыл дома кошелек!

Meaning: **Fuck**, I forgot my wallet at home!

Please don't confuse this word with **"блядь"** meaning **"a whore"** which is also used quite often. Both words sound the same, but they are not. The word **"блядь"** can be used to actually mean **"a whore"** or when you just want to insult a woman.

Example: Слышь ты **блядь**! Хватит на меня орать!

Meaning: Listen you **whore**! Stop yelling at me!

3. Сука блять [suka blyat] - famous curse phrase!

Now that we just discussed each word separately, let's reveal what the title of this book **"Cyka blyat!"** means.

Сука means **"bitch"** while блять is a multifunctional vulgarity along the lines of **"shit"** or **"fuck."** Together, **сука блять** is used to express uncontrollable anger, similar to dropping a series of F-bombs in English.

Example: Меня убили в Counter Strike! **Сука блять**!

Meaning: I got killed in Counter Strike! **Fucking shit!**

4. Выёбываться [vi-yO-bi-vat'-sya] - curse verb

This is also a very popular word in Russia, and actually, this word means **"to show off"**, **"think too much of yourself"**. The Russians usually use it jokingly or when arguing.

Let me show you examples of both ways so that you understand how to use it better.

First, in a joking way.

Example: — Моя машина круче твоей. — Хаха, не **выёбывайся**!

Meaning: — My car is better than yours. — Haha, don't **show off!**

Now, an aggressive way.

Example: Ты слишком много выёбываешься! Ты кем себя возомнил?

Meaning: You **think too much of yourself**! Who do you think you are?

5. Доебаться [da-ye-bAt'-sya] - curse verb

This word is super popular as well and is used in many situations, mostly in groups of friends or relatives. The actual meaning of it is **"to pester", "to bother"**.

Example: — Дай свой номер. — Я же уже сказала нет, чего **доебался**?

Meaning: — Give me your number! — I've told you no, why are you **pestering** me?

6. Ебало [ye-bA-la] - curse word

This is a super rude word that means **"a face"**. It is rarely used in comic situations, but more in rude ones.

Example: — Я вчера вообще не пил алкоголь. — Ну конечно, ты видел свое **ебало**?

Meaning: — I did not drink alcohol yesterday at all. — Of course, have you seen your **face**?

Another example: Хватит на меня орать или ударю тебя по **ебалу**!

Meaning: Stop yelling at me or I'll hit you in a **face**!

7. Ебнуть [yO-bnut'] - curse verb

This word has always been funny to me. It is frequently used in joking situations, but not only of course. The actual meaning of this curse verb is **"to hit"**, **"to beat someone/something"**

Example: Я ему вчера так **ебнул** за то, что он много сплетничает.

Meaning: I **hit** him so hard yesterday because he gossiped a lot.

There is another meaning of the word **"ебнуть"**, which is **"to drink"**. Many Russian men use this word as a toast when they drink alcohol.

Example: Наливай водку! Давай **ебнем**!

Meaning: Pour some vodka! Let's **drink**!

8. **Заебать** [za-ye-bAt'] - curse verb

The meaning of this curse verb is **"to make someone tired/sick of you"**.

Example: Не пиши мне, ты меня **заебал**!

Meaning: Don't text me, I am fucking **sick of you**!

9. **Заебись** [za-ye-bis'] - curse word

A favorite word of the Russian people! Actually, this curse word has a positive meaning. It means **"cool"**, **"amazing"**, **"excellent"**.Russians use it when they are happy.

Example: Наконец-то я поеду в отпуск, **заебись**!

Meaning: At last, I will go on a vacation, **amazing**!

One more example: — Как прошли выходные? — **Заебись!**

Meaning: — How was your weekend? — **Excellent!**

10. **Ебануться** [ye-ba-nUt'-sya] - curse verb

This word can be used either as a verb or also as an interjection.

The literal meaning of it is **"crazy", "out of one's mind", "unbelievable"**.

Let me show you two examples of how to use it.

Example: — Пойдем гулять. — Ты **ебанулся**? Время 3 утра.

Meaning: — Let's go out. — Are you **crazy**? It's 3 am

Here is an example where we use this word as an interjection.

Example: Я потратил столько денег в Москве, **ебануться!**

Meaning: I spent so much money in Moscow, **unbelievable!**

11. **Пизда** [pis-dA] - curse word

Literally, this word translates as **"a cunt", "vagina"** and Russians call some girls this, but only in a negative way of course, when they want to insult a person.

Example: Эта **пизда** меня уже достала!

Meaning: That **cunt** pissed me off already!

Another example: У этой молодой красотки классная **пизда**!

Meaning: This young hottie has an amazing **vagina!**

There is one more very common meaning for the word "**пизда**" that Russian people use a lot. We use it when something bad happens or there is a "**bad situation**" or something is "**fucked up**". Let me give you an example.

Example: Ситуация с коронавирусом это полная **пизда**!

Meaning: The situation with coronavirus is **fucked up!**

12. **Пиздатый** [pis-dA-tiy] - curse adjective

After you just learned that "**пизда**" is an awful situation, it might be hard for you to understand, but the word "**пиздатый**" has a positive meaning! Russians say this word when they describe something or someone great. So the actual meaning is "**awesome**", "**great**", "**good quality**".

Example: Твоя новая машина просто **пиздатая**!

Meaning: Your new car is **fucking amazing**!

13. **Пиздец** [pis-dEc] - curse word

Russian people use this word often and it has the same meaning as the word "**пизда**" which is "**a bad situation**", "**something unpleasant**".

Example: Погода сегодня ужасная, просто **пиздец**!

Meaning: The weather is horrible today, just **bad**!

14. Пиздабол [pis-da-bOl] - slang adjective

The actual meaning of this slang word is **"a liar"**. This word has a negative meaning at first sight, but it is also used in comic situations sometimes.

Let me show you a couple of examples.

Example: — У него столько денег! — Не верь ему, он тот еще **пиздабол!**

Meaning: — He has got so much money! — Don't believe him, he is such **a lier!**

Another example (joking way): — Ты такая красивая! — Хаха, перестань, ты такой **пиздабол**!

Meaning: — You are so beautiful! — Haha, stop it, you are such **a liar!**

15. Поебень [pa-ye-bEn'] - slang word

Russians say this when they mean **"bullshit"**, **"nonsense"** etc. There are lots of situations where they might use it. It's suitable for everything.

Example: Хватит рассказывать мне эту **поебень** про свою жизнь.

Meaning: Stop telling me this **bullshit** about your life.

16. Распиздяй [ras-piz'-dyAi] (for a male) Распиздяйка [ras-piz'-dyAi-ka] (for a female) - curse word

That is a negative assessment or characteristic of a person which means **"irresponsible"**.

Sometimes, you can use it towards someone close to you, but only in a joking way, otherwise, it is going to start a quarrel.

First, I'll show you a negative way to use it.

Example: — Катя совсем не ходит в университет. — Да, она такая **распиздяйка**.

Meaning: — Kate never goes to class at the university. — Yes, she is such an **irresponsible person**.

Here is another example, but in a comic way.

Example: — Я сегодня проспал и не пошел на работу. — Ты безответственный **распиздяй**!

Meaning: — I overslept today and did not go to work. — You are an **irresponsible fuck.**

17. **Спиздить** [spis'-dit'] - curse verb

Literally, this word means **"to steal"**. Even though it is a curse word, it does not have a negative meaning, and you may bravely use it in the company of your close friends. But it is also very often used in negative situations. I will show you both variants of usage.

Positive way:

Example: — Ты опять **спиздила** мою юбку? — Да, мы же друзья

Meaning: Did you **steal** (here it means more like **"borrow"**) my skirt again? —Yes, we are friends after all.

Negative meaning:

Example: Кто-то **спиздил** мой телефон!

Meaning: Someone **stole** my phone!

18. **Хуйня** [huy-nyA] - curse word

This word has a couple of meanings. First, it can describe things or experiences, like bad-quality stuff or something unpleasant. Another meaning is **"nonsense"**, **"something that is not important"**, or **"no problem"**. I will show you examples now.

The first variant of usage:

Example: — Ну как тебе фильм? — Если честно, это такая **хуйня**.

Meaning: — So how did you like the movie? — To be honest, it was such **bullshit**.

The second variant of usage:

Example: — Прости, я толкнул тебя. — **Хуйня.**

Meaning: — Sorry, I pushed you. — **No problem.**

But do not use it in either way if the person who you are talking to is not someone you know well.

19. **В пизду** [f pis-dU] - curse phrase

Actually, literally speaking, the translation of this phrase is **"to the cunt"**, but that doesn't make sense, right? So now, I will explain what Russians actually mean.

There are a couple of different meanings. The first one we use when we mean **"fuck it"**!

Example: Я не могу сделать этот проект уже два часа, **в пизду** его!

Meaning: I haven't been able to get my project done for two hours, **fuck it!**

Another popular meaning of this curse phrase is **"fuck off"**. It is very commonly used by Russians when they argue with each other!

Example: Ты мне надоел! Иди **в пизду!**

Meaning: I'm so tired of you! **Fuck off!**

20. **Нахуй** [nA-huy] - curse word

This word has two different meanings, depending on the situation. Now, I will help you figure out how and when to use it.

The first meaning used by Russians is **"why the fuck"**, **"what for"**. So it is more like a question.

Example: — Я снова хочу встречаться с Игорем. — **Нахуй?** Он же идиот!

Meaning: — I want to date Igor again. — **Why the fuck?** He is an idiot!

Another meaning is used in the phrase **"иди нахуй"** which translates as **"go to the dick"**. This is another way to say **"fuck off"**, **"go fuck yourself"**. Actually, it has exactly the same meaning as the phrase **"в пизду"** that we just discussed. You are probably very confused right now, asking yourself why Russians always try to send someone to a man's dick or a woman's vagina. I don't have an explanation! But here are a few examples:

Example: — Займи мне денег. — **Иди нахуй**, ты мне никогда не отдаешь их обратно!

Meaning: — Lend me some money. — **Go fuck yourself**, you never give it back to me!

Another example: — Красотка, давай проведем ночь вместе! — **Иди нахуй!**

Meaning: — Hey beautiful, let's spend a night together! — **Fuck off!**

21. Уёбок [u-yO-bak] - curse word

This is a funny, but at the same time, rude word. The meaning of it is **"a loser", "an idiot", "a bad person"**. You may insult someone with this word, but friends also commonly call each other this when joking.

Negative example: Ты тупая курица. Как ты назвал меня, ты **уёбок?**

Meaning: You are a stupid chick. What did you call me, are you **an idiot?**

Positive example: — У меня нет денег сводить тебя в ресторан. — У тебя вечно нет денег, **уёбок,** хаха!

Meaning: — I don't have money to take you to the restaurant. — You never have money, **loser**, haha!

22. Мне похуй [mne pO-huy] - curse phrase

This phrase means **"I don't fucking care", "fuck it"**. Russians love using it.

Example: — Если ты не извинишься, я не буду с тобой разговаривать. — **Мне похуй**.

Meaning: — If you do not apologize, I will not talk to you. — **I don't fucking care**.

You can just say one word **"похуй"** to express the same meaning.

Example: Я потерял работу, ну и **похуй**.

Meaning: I lost my job, well **fuck it**.

23. Охуенный (for males) [ahu-yEn-niy] **охуенная** [ahu-yEn-na-ya] (for females) - curse adjective

This word has no literal translation in English, but actually, it means **"fucking awesome", "amazing", "super cool"**. It has a positive meaning most of the time. But if you want to compliment a girl you don't really know, you better not use this word.

Example: — Видел новую девушку у Николая? — Да, она просто **охуенная!**

Meaning: — Have you seen Nikolay's new girlfriend? — Yes, she is **fucking awesome!**

However, there are some situations where we use it in a sarcastic way to describe something not so awesome.

Example: Я только что разбил свою машину. Вот **охуенно!**

Meaning: I just crashed my car. It's **fucking great!**

24. **Ебанутый** [ye-ba-nU-tiy] - curse adjective

The literal meaning of this curse word is **"fucking crazy", "dumb", "an idiot".**

Example: — Ты знала, что он каждый день ругается с женой? — Да, он вообще **ебанутый.**

Meaning: — Did you know he argues with his wife daily? — Yes, he is **fucking crazy.**

Another example: Он спустил все сбережения в казино. Вот **идиот**!

Meaning: He spent all his savings at the casino. Such **an idiot**!

25. **Заёба** [za-yO-ba] - curse word

This is what Russians call **"tedious"** people that piss everyone off. Or it could also mean **"a bore"**.

You can call your friend this jokingly as well, but do not forget it is not always funny and can be offensive.

Let me show you both negative and positive examples.

Negative example: — Почему вы больше не зовете его с нами гулять? — Потому что он жуткий **заёба.**

Meaning: — Why don't you invite him to hang out with us anymore? — Because he is **a bore.**

Positive example: — Я сегодня не приду к тебе. — Еще как придешь, не будь **заёбой**!

Meaning: — I will not come over tonight. — Of course you will, do not be **a bore**.

26. Подъебать [pat-ye-bAt'] - curse verb

This slang verb means **"to laugh at someone", "to tease", "to make fun of someone"**. This verb is often used among friends in comic situations.

Example: — Ну и где же твоя красивая девушка с которой ты обещал нас познакомить? — Мы расстались и не **подъебывай** меня.

Meaning: — Where is your beautiful girlfriend you promised to introduce us to? — We broke up and do not **make fun of me** now.

27. Заёбанный [za-yO-ban-niy] - curse adjective

Russian people use this adjective when they mean **"tired", "exhausted", "sad"**.

Example: — Он работает целыми днями. — Да, по нему видно какой он **заёбанный**.

Meaning: — He works all day long. — Yes, I can see how **exhausted** he is.

28. Ебать мозги [e-bAt' maz-gi] - curse phrase

The literal translation of this phrase is **"to fuck brains"** and it means **"to annoy someone"**.

Example: — Почему Катя и Макс расстались? — Она слишком много **ебала** ему **мозги**.

Meaning: — Why did Kate and Max break up? — She **annoyed** him too much.

29. **Ебать** [e-bAt'] - slang verb

This is actually a very rude word. The translation is **"to fuck"** and I guess you already understood it means **"to have sex"** but in a harsh way.

Example: Саша предложил Насте **поебаться** и она отказала ему.

Meaning: Sasha asked Nastya **to fuck** with him, but she refused.

30. **Наебнуться** [na-ye-bnU-t'sya] - curse verb

This word has no translation in English, but it means **"to fall down"**. It is a very hilarious word and there are many situations where Russians use this curse word.

Example: — Где ты порвал свои джинсы? — Я подскользнулся и **наебнулся** по дороге.

Meaning: — Where did you tear up your jeans? — I slipped and **fell down** on the ground.

31. **Проебать** [pra-ye-bAt'] - curse verb

The actual meaning of this word is **"to lose something"**, **"to waste"**, **"to spend"**.

Example: Я опять **проебал** свои деньги в баре!

Meaning: I **spent** all my money at the bar again!

Another example: Я **проебал** шанс познакомиться с ней!

Meaning: I **lost** a chance to meet her!

32. **Наебать** [na-ye-bAt'] - curse verb

This word looks and sounds similar to the previous one but it has a completely different meaning. This one means **"to fool someone", "to trick"**.

Example: — Скинь мне сначала деньги, а я тебе отправлю продукт. — **Наебать** меня решил?

Meaning: — Send me the money first, and then I will send you the product. — Did you decide **to fool** me?

33. **Уёбывать** [u-yO-bi-vat'] - slang verb

This verb does not have an insulting intention, but it is still a curse word. The meaning of it is **"to go away fast", "to run away"**.

Example: Они нас узнали, нам пора **уёбывать**!

Meaning: They recognized us, it's time **to run away**!

34. **Поебень** [pa-ye-bEn'] - curse word

This word means **"nonsense", "bullshit", 'something with bad-quality"**.

Example: Мне не понравились твои сигареты, не предлагай мне больше такую **поебень**!

Meaning: I did not like your cigarettes, don't offer me **shit** like that again.

35. Ебанный [yO-ban-niy] - curse adjective

This word is used to describe a bad situation or a person. It means **"shitty", "bad", "horrible", "fucking"**.

Example: Я больше не пойду в этот **ебанный** клуб, я оставил там все свои деньги вчера!

Meaning: I will never go to that **fucking** nightclub again, I spent all my money there yesterday!

Another example: Что за **ебанный** день был вчера! Я потерял работу!

Meaning: What a **horrible** day I had yesterday! I lost my job!

36. Разъебать [ras-ye-bAt'] - curse verb

The literal meaning of this verb is to **"to crush", "to break something"**.

Example: — Твой телефон выглядит ужасно. — Да я его **разъебал**.

Meaning: — Your cellphone looks awful. — Yeah, I **crushed** it.

37. Хуй [huy] - curse word

Actually, the translation of this word is **"a dick", "a cock"** and we use it this way very often. But there are a couple of other meanings that Russian people use this word for.

1) as a way to insult like "**a fool**", "**an idiot**"

2) a harsh way to refuse like **"fuck no"**

Example 1: Этот **хуй** меня раздражает!

Meaning: That **idiot** annoys me!

Example 2: — Займи денег. — **Хуй.**

Meaning: — Lend me money. — **Fuck no.**

38. Хули [hU-li] - curse word

This word has no correct translation, but it means **"why the fuck"?**

Example: **Хули** ты так много раз звонил мне, я же тебе сказал я сплю!

Meaning: **Why the fuck** did you call me so many times, I told you I was sleeping!

39. Хуй там плавал [huy tam plA-val] - curse phrase

One of the funniest and most confusing phrases, the literal translation of it is **"penis swam there"** but it means **"there is nothing all".**

Example: — Начальник уже заплатил тебе? — **Хуй там плавал**

Meaning: — Did your boss pay you already? — **Nope**

40. Хуяк [hu-yAk] - curse word

This is a funny interjection. It means **"bang"**, **"zap"**, **"boom"**.

Example: — Откуда у тебя такая шишка на лбу? — Сидел под деревом и **хуяк**, яблоко упало на голову!

Meaning: — How did you get such a bump on your forehead? — I was sitting under a tree and **boom**, an apple fell on my head!

41. **Нихуя себе** [ni-hu-yA si-be] - curse phrase

This is also an interjection that is used to express your emotions when you are surprised or amazed. It would be like **"wow"** in English.

Example: **Нихуя себе** какая классная у тебя девчонка!

Meaning: **Wow** what a cute girl you've got!

Another example: **Нихуя себе** какая старая у тебя куртка!

Meaning: **Wow** what an old coat you have!

42. **Хуйло** [hUy-lo] - curse word

The meaning of this word is **"dumbass", "idiot", "jerk"**.

Example: — Катя, он меня бросил! — Не переживай, Аня, он всегда был то еще **хуйло.**

Meaning: — Kate, he dump me! — Don't worry, Ann, he was always **a jerk**.

43. **Хуеплет** [hu-ye-plyOt] - curse word

This word also describes a person and it means **"a person who lies and shows off too much without any proofs".**

Example: — Я вам покажу свой большой дом и машину. — Да-да, мы не верим, ты такой **хуеплет**!

Meaning: — I will show you my huge house and car. — Yeah yeah, we don't believe you, you are such **a liar**!

44. **Тянуть за хуй** [tya-nUt' za huy] - curse phrase

The literal translation of this phrase is **"to pull the cock"**. It actually means **"to do something slowly"**, **"procrastinate"**, **"waste time"**.

Example: Сделай уже свою домашнюю работу, ты всю неделю **тянешь за хуй**!

Meaning: Get your homework done already, you've been **procrastinating** for a week!

Another example: Пора перестать **тянуть за хуй** и действовать!

Meaning: It's time to stop **wasting time** and act!

Many people say **"тянуть за яйца"** which you can translate as **"to pull the balls"** and has the same meaning as **"тянуть за хуй"**.

Example: Говори скорей, хватит **тянуть за яйца**!

Meaning: Tell me quickly, stop **wasting time**!

45. **Спиздануть** [spi-zda-nUt'] - curse verb

This verb means **"to say something by accident"** or **"say something without thinking"**

Example: — Я назвал Аню толстой и она обиделась. — Ты любишь **спиздануть**, не подумав.

Meaning: — I called Ann fat and she got offended. — You love to **say things without thinking**.

46. **Пиздовать** [pis-da-vAt'] - curse verb

This slang verb means **"to walk", "to go".**

Example: Уже поздно, пора **пиздовать**.

Meaning: It is late already, it's time **to go**.

Another example: Я видел как ты и Аня **пиздовали** в сторону магазина.

Meaning: I saw you and Ann **walking** to the store.

So, guys, these were the most popular and widely used curse words in Russia! Of course, there are many more, but I made sure to select the best ones. Russian curse language differs from the curse words of other countries because in general, the Russian language is harder to learn. But don't worry I am here to help you.

P.S. Not all Russians use these words on a daily basis and even if most of them do, they only do so in suitable places and situations.

CHAPTER 9

Russian slang derived from the English

I think I've told you enough about Russian slang words. However, there are also slang words that were derived from the English language! You can easily recognize them by their pronunciation.

They are mostly used among teenagers and youngsters, but you need to know them before going to Russia, anyway, because you will hear them everywhere!

1. **Хайп** [hype] - slang word

This word comes from the English word **"hype"** and it actually has the same meaning in Russian.

The word **"hype"** means excitement around something, something fashionable at the moment.

There is also a verb that comes from this word which is **"хайпить"**, which means **"to hype"**.

Example: — Ты видел какие фото она выложила в фейсбук? — Да, она просто **хайпиться.**

Meaning: — Have you seen the pictures she posted on her Facebook? —Yes, she just trying to get a **hype** around her.

2. **Рилли** - [really] slang word

This word comes from the English word **"really"**. Our youth uses it as a synonym for the words **"truth"**, **"real"**, and sometimes instead of the word **"very"** or **"truly"**. It is also often used as a surprised question in reaction to a story, or to exaggerate something.

Example: — Ты знал что каникулы продлили? — **Рилли**?

Meaning: — Did you know they made our vacation longer? — **Really**?

Another example: Она **рилли** очень красивая.

Meaning: She is **truly** very beautiful.

3. **Чиллить** [chIl-lit'] - slang verb

This word comes from the expression in English **"to chill"**. Russians use it to mean **"to relax", "spend time"**. Sometimes it is used to mean **"to party"**.

Example: — Что делаете сегодня вечером, девочки? — **Чиллим** у Кати.

Meaning: — What are you doing tonight, girls? — We are **chilling** at Kate's place.

4. **Шазамить** [sha-zA-mit'] - slang verb

There is an app for smartphones, called Shazam, that recognizes what song is currently playing. So **"шазамить"** means **"to find out the name of a song using this or a similar app"**.

Example: О, я обожаю эту песню, надо срочно ее **зашазамить.**

Meaning: Oh, I love this song, I need to **shazam** it right now.

5. Изи [easy] - slang adjective

It comes from the English word **"easy"**. Most often, it is used to refer to some kind of incredibly simple task or express a person's attitude towards different life situations. It can also be used to ask someone to "**take it easy"** or **"calm down".**

Example: — Ну как прошла контрольная? — Ой вообще **изи**, я быстро написал ее.

Meaning: — How was your test? — Ah, it was **easy**, I finished it quickly.

Another example: — Я не контролирую себя когда злой. — **Изи**, бро.

Meaning: — I am not able to control myself when I am mad. — **Calm down**, bro

6. Агриться [Ag-rit'-sya] - slang verb

There are 2 versions of the origin of this word: either from the English word **"angry"** or from the word **"aggression"**. Teenagers use this word as a synonym for the words **"angry", "freaking out", "hating".**

Example: — Я вообще не хочу с тобой разговаривать. —Перестань **агриться** на меня.

Meaning: — I don't want to talk to you at all. — Stop **being angry** at me.

7. **Го** [go] - slang verb

In English, the verb to **"go"** sounds like **"гоу" (goʊ)**. But today's youth is lazy and likes to use short words in both speech and writing. Even the word **"goʊ"** turned out to be too long for them, so it was reduced to just **"го" (go)**. Russians use this word when they want to invite each other somewhere or suggest doing something.

Example: — **Го** сегодня гулять? — **Го.**

Meaning: — Let's **go** out tonight? — Go. (which means okay)

8. **Шеймить** [shEi-mit'] - slang verb

"Шеймить" comes from the English word **"to shame"**, and it is used when people want to shame a person for something. For example, for a style of clothes or an act. The derivative from this word is **"шеймеры"** - **"shamers"**. **"Шеймеры"** are people who abuse others.

Example: Люди всегда **шеймили** ее за странный стиль в одежде, но в итоге она стала знаменитостью.

Meaning: People used **to shame** her for a weird style in clothes, but eventually, she became a celebrity.

9. **Соррян** [sar'-yAn] - slang word

This slang word comes from the English word **"sorry"**. That's what people say when they apologize. It's funny that the word **"сорри"** has been used for many years in Russian speech along with the Russian words **"извини"** and "прости", but for some reason, this very "сорри" mutated and turned into an even more careless "соррян".

For example: — Ты наступил мне на ногу! — **Соррян.**

Meaning: — You stepped on my foot! — **Sorry.**

10. **Рофл** [rofl] - slang word

"**Рофл**" or "**ROFL**" is an English abbreviation for the phrase **"rolling on the floor laughing"**. In the past, when communicating through some instant messengers, people used an emoji, which rolled on the floor laughing. Now, "**Рофл**" means "**laugh out loud**" or "**play a joke on someone**". Among teenagers, this word is also used in the meaning of **"insanely funny joke or story"**.

Example: — Вчера я был настолько пьян, что потерял свои джинсы. — Хаха, это просто **рофл**.

Meaning: — Yesterday I was so drunk that I lost my jeans. — Haha, it is a real **ROFL.**

One more example: Хочешь расскажу **рофл**?

Meaning: Do you want to hear **a funny joke**?

11. **Гамать** [ga-mAt'] - slang verb

It comes from the English word **"game"**. Russian teenagers use this word when they mean to **"spend time playing a computer game"**.

Example: Будешь сегодня вечером **гамать** со мной?

Meaning: Will you **play a video game** with me tonight?

12. Чекать [chE-kat'] - slang verb

It comes from the English word **"to check"** and it means **"to check information about something or someone"**.

Example: — Ты видела его новые фотки с девушкой? — Нет еще, сейчас **чекну**.

Meaning: — Have you seen his new pictures with his girlfriend? — Not yet, let me **check**.

13. Хейтить [hEi-tit'] - slang verb

This slang word comes from the English word **"to hate"**. When Russians say it, they mean **"can't stand someone or something"**, well, just the same meaning as in English. People that hate someone are called **"хейтерс"** which obviously comes from the word **"haters"**.

Example: — Почему Аня и Катя больше не дружат? — Кажется, они поссорились и теперь **хейтят** друг друга.

Meaning: — Why aren't Ann and Kate friends anymore? — I guess, they argued and now they **hate** each other.

14. Плизки [plis-ki] - slang word

This slang word comes from the English word **"please"** and is used just in the same situations as English speakers use it.

Example: Дай мне **плизки** свой номер.

Meaning: Give me your number, **please**.

15. Лузер [lU-zer] - slang word

This word comes from the English word **"loser"**. When Russian people say this word, they mean **"an unsuccessful person"**. Russian teens like using it in comic situations as well. Let me show you both variations of usage.

Negative way.

Example: — Он проиграл все деньги. — Да, он тот еще **лузер.**

Meaning: — He lost all his money. — Yes, he is such **a loser**.

Positive way.

Example: — Я запачкала свои джинсы. — Ну ты лузер, хаха!

Meaning: — I messed my jeans up. — Haha, what **a loser** you are!

16. **Дэнсить** [dEn'-cit'] - slang verb

This one comes from the English **"to dance"** and actually has the same meaning in Russian. The Russian youth likes using it when they mean to go partying etc.

Example: — Как прошла вчера вечеринка? — Классно, мы много **дэнсили.**

Meaning: — How was the party yesterday? — It was cool, we **danced** a lot.

17. **Фэйл** [fail] - slang word

This word comes from **"to fail", "a failure"** and means **"to not succeed in what you are trying to achieve or are expected to do"**.

Example: — Ты видела как Аня забыла слова во время выступления? — Да, это был фэйл.

Meaning: —Did you see how Ann forgot the words during her performance? — Yes, it was such **a failure**.

18. **Топчик** [tOp-chik] - slang word

Originally, the word comes from English **"top"** which means **"the best", "greatest"** etc. In Russia, young people just use this word to express that something is good.

Example: — Как тебе мое новое платье? — Просто **топчик**!

Meaning: — How do you like my new dress? —Simply **the best**!

19. **Хаюшки** [hA-yu-shki] - slang word

A deformed word from the English word **"hi"**, usually, only teens use this word in a group of friends. Sometimes, they use just **"хай"** which is not deformed at all.

Example: Здравствуй! **Хаюшки**!

Meaning: Hello! Hi!

20. **Лук** [look] - slang word

This word has the same meaning as the English word **"look"** or **"outfit"**. It is a very popular word not only among teens but also in social media, magazines, among bloggers, etc.

Example: — Классный **лук**! Куда так нарядилась? — На свидание.

Meaning: — Great **outfit**! Why did you dress so well today? — I am going on a date.

21. **Мейкап** [make-up] - slang word

This one literally comes from the English word **"makeup"** and has absolutely the same meaning.

Example: У Ани такой вульгарный **мейкап** сегодня.

Meaning: Ann is wearing such vulgar **makeup** today.

22. **Мастхэв** [must-have] - slang word

It comes from the English word **"must-have"** and actually means **"necessary"**, **"essential"**.

Example: — У меня нет крема для загара. — Как это нет? Это же **мастхэв** для отпуска!

Meaning: — I don't have a sunscreen cream. — How do you not? It's a **must-have** for vacation!

23. **Тренд** [trend] - slang word

The same word as the English word **"trend"**, it literally has the same meaning and ways of usage.

Example: — Вау, классные у тебя очки! — Спасибо, это **тренд**.

Meaning: — Wow, what a cool pair of sunglasses you have! — Thanks, it's a **trend**.

24. **Прайс** [price] - slang word

This word comes from the English word **"price"** and the Russians frequently use it in their everyday life just in the same way as English speakers do.

Example: — Добро пожаловать в наш салон красоты. — Могу я ознакомиться с **прайсом**?

Meaning: — Welcome to our beauty salon. — May I see the **prices**?

Another example: — Купил себе новый телефон. — Что по **прайсу**?

Meaning: — I bought a new smartphone. — What's the **price**?

25. **Сингл** [single] - slang word

This word comes from the English **"a single"** in the meaning of a song only.

Example: У Рианны вышел новый **сингл**, ты уже слышала?

Meaning: Rihanna's new **single** is out, have you already heard?

26. **Экшн** [action] - slang word

This one comes from the English word **"action"**. When Russian people use this word, they mean that there is " **something going on"**, **"something exciting"**.

Example: — Ты знала, что Никита и Влад подрались? — Да, я видела их драку, это был **экшн**!

Meaning: — Did you know Nikita and Vlad had a fight? — Yes, I saw it, it was an "**action!**"

27. Эпик [epic] - slang word

This word comes from the English word **"epic"** and is rarely used by the older generation, even though young people like this word.

Example: — Аня снова сошлась с Максимом! —Да, это просто **эпик**!

Meaning: — Ann got back together with Maxim again! — Yeah, it is just **epic**!

28. Хэндмэйд [hand-made] - slang word

This word is just a Russian version of the English word **"hand-made"**, Russians use it when they want to say that something is made by hand.

Example: — Вау, какое милое у тебя кольцо. — Спасибо, это **хэнд-мейд.**

Meaning: — Wow, you have such a nice ring. — Thanks, it's **hand-made**.

29. Трэш [trash] - slang word

Just like the previous words, this one comes directly from an English word **"trash"** which means **"shit, "garbage", "junk"** and is used by Russian teens to describe something unpleasant or shitty.

Example: Новая коллекция в этом магазине просто **трэш**.

Meaning: The new collection at this shop is just **trash**.

30. **Селебрити** [celebrity] - slang word

This word comes from the English word **"celebrity"** and has the same meaning. It is used often by Russian teens.

Example: Обожаю фильм Титаник, там снимаются все мои любимые **селебрити**.

Meaning: I adore the Titanic movie because all my favorite **celebrities** are in it.

31. **Уик-енд** [weekend] - slang word

This word comes from the English word **"weekend"** and literally means the end of the week, just like in English.

Example: — Как провела **уик-енд**? — Неплохо, отдыхала дома.

Meaning: — How was your **weekend**? — Not bad, I relaxed at home.

32. **Мани** [money] - slang word

This word comes from the English word **"money"** and is used in the same way. Russians love this word.

Example: **Мани** есть в долг?

Meaning: Have you got some **money** to lend?

33. **Окей** [ok] - slang word

This is one of the most used words in Russia and it has been used in Russian people's speech for many years, so they don't even notice anymore that this word is not Russian at all.

It comes from the English word **"okay"** and has the same meaning and is used in the same way.

Example: — Не забудь купить молока! — **Окей**.

Meaning: — Don't forget to buy milk! — **Okay**.

34. **Респект** [respect] - slang word

This word has also been used in Russian speech for many years and feels "Russian" but that is not true. This word comes from the English word **"respect"**. The Russians have another word with the same meaning, but these days a lot of people use **"респект"** instead.

Example: — Я позвал Юлю на свидание и она согласилась. — **Респект** тебе, чувак!

Meaning: — I asked Julia out and she agreed. — **Respect** to you, dude!

35. **Загуглить** [za-gU-glit'] - slang verb

This word is deformed from the English **"to search something in Google"** or simply **"to Google"**. This is a very popular verb among Russians, and not only teenagers.

Example: — Сколько зубов у акулы? — Не знаю, **загугли**.

Meaning: — How many teeth do sharks have? — I don't know, **google it**.

36. **Зачекиниться** [za-che-kI-nit'-sya] - slang verb

This word is deformed from the English **"to check in"** and actually means **"to check in"** or sometimes **"to sign in to some site"**.

Example: Как **зачекиниться** на сайте с Айфона?

Meaning: How do I **sign in** from an iPhone?

Another example: Мне надо позвонить Маше **зачекиниться**, чтобы она не волновалась.

Meaning: I have to call and **check in** with Masha, so she doesn't worry.

37. **Хэлп** [help] - slang word

This word comes from the English word **"help"** and has the same meaning. Young people use this word a lot.

Example: Не могу сделать домашку, **хэлп**!

Meaning: I can't do my homework, **help**!

38. **Сириосли** [seriously] - slang word

This word comes from the English word **"seriously"**. Just like many of the previous words, it has the same meaning and is used in the same way as the original English word.

Example: — Я переезжаю в другой город. — **Сириосли**?

Meaning: — I am moving to another city. — **Seriously**?

39. **Апргрейднуть** [ap-grEyd-nut'] - slang verb

This word comes from the English verb **"to upgrade"** which means **"to modernize"** both in Russian and in English.

Example: Я решил **апргейднуть** свою внешность и стиль.

Meaning: I decided **to upgrade** my appearance and style.

40. **Олды** [al-dI] - slang word

This word is popular mostly among teenagers and comes from the English word **"old"**. Whenever Russians discuss something from the past like old household items, frames from old films, or music collections of the past, they use this word. They also use it to refer to old newspapers and magazines that evoke emotions among those who lived at that time.

41. **Фейк** [fake] - slang adjective

This word comes from the English word **"fake"** which means **"not real", "not true", "imitation"**.

Example: — У тебя настоящие джинсы Луи Виттон? — Нет, это **фейк**.

Meaning: — Are your Louis Vuitton jeans real? — Nope, they are **fake**.

42. Спойлерить [spOy-le-rit'] - slang verb

This word comes from the English **"spoiler"**. It means telling the outcome of events, destroying intrigue, or spoiling something (like a movie) for a person who has not yet seen or has not used what is being talked about. As a result, a person loses interest in the "thing" and may intentionally skip reading, watching, or using it.

Example: — Ты знаешь что будет в следующей серии? — Нет и не **спойлери** мне!

Meaning: — Do you know what happens in the next episode? No and don't **spoil** it for me!

43. Пранковать [pran-ko-vAt'] - slang verb

This word comes from the English **"to prank"** which means **"to make fun of someone"**, **"to joke"** etc.

Example: — Почему Настя не разговаривает с тобой? — Я над ней неудачно **пранканул**.

Meaning: — Why Nastya is not talking to you? — I pranked her unsuccessfully.

43. Прувы [prU-vi] - slang word

This word comes from the English word **"proof"**. This word is not the most used one, but I decided to add include it in this chapter, because I've heard teenagers say it many times, so I thought you should know it as well.

Example: Мне нужны **прувы**, что ты меня не обманешь.

Meaning: I need **proofs** that you are not going to fool me.

So, my dear Russian admirers, there was the list of the most popular slang words that have come from English! It is not surprising though, we live in the century of globalization and English is an international language. Moreover, many of these words have been in the Russian language for many years, but a few of them are new. I am sure that with time, they will take root in Russia as well.

Lucky for you though! It will help you easily learn more slang words when you travel to Russia!

CHAPTER 10

Confusing Russian slang phrases

The Russian language is incredible. The same words can mean completely different things and express completely opposite emotions. The fact that words can be used so differently can often leave a foreigner confused. Here in my review, I want to show you guys some examples which will prove to you that the Russian language is really interesting and not that simple.

Let's start!

1. **Да нет, наверное** [da net na-vEr-na-ye]

No, these are not just three different words which are not connected with each other. It is actually a phrase. Now I will explain to you that **"да"** means **"yes"**, **"нет"** means "**no**", and "**наверное**"means "**maybe**". So if we link them together, we get **"yes no maybe"** and now I bet I made you absolutely confused. How could a phrase like this even mean anything?

But actually, it is a very popular and frequently used phrase among Russians and it simply means **"probably not"**.

For example: — Ты зайдешь сегодня ко мне? — **Да нет наверное**, уже поздно.

Meaning: — Will you come over tonight? — **Probably not**, it is late.

2. Стоять над душой [sta-yAt' nat du-shOy]

The translation of this phrase is something like **"to stand over someone's soul"**. Sounds kinda creepy, doesn't it? But actually, the meaning of it is not creepy at all, and it is very close to the English phrase **"to breathe down someone's neck"**. Russians say it when someone is relentlessly, annoyingly asking or demanding something from someone or just annoying with their presence.

Example: — Ну давай я помогу тебе с домашним заданием. — Нет , я уже сто раз сказала, **не стой на душой**!

Meaning: — Please, let me help you with your home work! — No, I've told you a hundred times already, **stop breathing down my neck!**

3. Давай пока [da-vAy pa-kA]

This phrase consists of two words that are not connected with each other by their meaning. Literally "**давай**" means "**give**", and "**пока**" means "**bye**".

So here we have , **"give bye"**. I know that all of this can be very confusing for you, but actually Russian people, when using this phrase, just mean **"bye"**.

For example: — Пока, увидимся. — **Давай пока.**

Meaning: — Bye, see you. — **Bye**.

4. Ноги в руки [nO-gi v rU-ki]

The literal translation of this phrase is **"legs to arms"**. It is used to express the need to immediately go somewhere or do something, or to tell someone they need to "just do it." The closest translation in English would be **"go do it", "go ahead".**

Example: — Я так хочу заработать много денег. — **Ноги в руки** и вперед работать!

Meaning: — I want to earn lots of money. — **Go ahead** and start working! (Well then, just start!)

5. **Потому что** [pa-ta-mUsh-ta]

This phrase means **"because"** and now you are probably wondering, what's special and surprising about this phrase? Be patient, dear reader. This word is simple when you use it while explaining something to someone, but Russian people like to use it as an answer. Let me explain with the help of an example so that you can better understand.

Example: — Аня, почему ты обиделась? — **Потому что**!

Meaning: — Ann, why are you offended? — **Because!** (and yes guys, it's a complete answer, there is no continuation. This answer means "**someone does not want to reply or you need to figure it out by yourself why she got offended".**

6. **Ничего** [Ni-chi-vO]

The literal translation of this word is **"nothing"**. However, the most popular meaning is **"not bad"**. So now you know this and won't be confused, but I am sure most travelers do get confused when hearing this.

Example: — Как прошли выходные? — **Ничего**, а как у тебя?

Meaning: — How was your weekend? — **Not bad**, and yours?

7. **Когда рак на горе свистнет** [kog-dA rak na ga-rE svI-st-net]

The literal translation of this phrase is **"when the cancer will whistle on the mountain"** which means **"never"**. Writing all of that for you guys reminds me once again how funny and at the same time difficult the Russian language is.

Example: — Когда уже сменишь свою дурацкую прическу? — **Когда рак на горе свистнет.**

Meaning: — When will you change your freaky ridiculous hairstyle? — **Never.**

8. — Ты куда? — Я ненадолго!

— **Where are you going? — Not for long!** [ti ku-da? Ya ne-na-dO-lga]

Only in Russia, can one respond to a specific question about the direction of one's movement, by providing only the expected amount of time of one's absence, and this will be perceived by the asker as absolutely normally. The paradox is that this answer will be enough for a Russian person, but how to explain this to a foreigner?

9. — **Почему?** — **По кочану!** [pa-chi-mU? pa-ka-chi-nU]

Le me explain what the answer **"по кочану"** means when someone asks the question **"почему"** which means **"why"**. **"Кочан"** means a head of cabbage. So **"по качену"** is literally **"on the head of cabbage"**. However, if we say it about a person's head we mean this person is stupid. What does it mean in our phrase? We mean **"don't ask me this you stupid"** or just **"none of your business"**. Uhhh, so confusing, I know!

Example: — Почему ты не пришел на встречу? — **Покочану!**

Meaning: — Why didn't you come to a meeting? — **None of your business!**

10. **Ничего себе!** [ni-chi-vO si-bE]

Actually, the direct translation of this phrase is **"nothing for myself"**, but the real meaning is **"wow", "whoa", "surprising".**

Example: — Я купил БМВ. — **Ничего себе!**

Meaning: — I bought a BMW. — **Wow!**

11. **Будешь?** [bU-desh]

The translation of this word is **"will you?"**, but it is usually used just to offer something to someone.

One American woman admitted that it was extremely difficult for her to understand why we use this verb to mean **"want"**.

Example: **Будешь** чай? **Будешь** шоколад?

Meaning: **Do you want** some tea? **Do you want** some chocolate?

She honestly admitted that she still does not fully understand why we say it this way. Well, girl...we also don't always understand why we say some words!

12. Холод собачий [hO-lad sa-bA-chiy]

The translation of this phrase is **"the dog's cold"** with **"cold"** referring to a low temperature, not the flu.

We do not know why the word dog is used here, actually when Russians say it, it has nothing to do with dogs. This phrase simply means **"very cold"**.

Example: —Пойдем гулять? —Я в такой **собачий холод** никуда не пойду.

Meaning: —Let's go for a walk? — I'm not going anywhere, it's **very cold**.

13. Старый Новый год [stA-riy nO-viy got]

The translation of this phrase is **"the Old New Year"**.

The tradition of celebrating the Old New Year arose after the introduction of the Gregorian calendar in 1918, as a result of which January 1st, according to the Julian calendar, began to correspond to January 14th, according to the adopted Gregorian calendar.

14. Молоко убежало [ma-la-kO u-bi-zhA-lo]

This is a funny phrase that translates as **"milk ran away"**. To me it sounds pretty funny, but it actually means that **"milk spilled or boiled over"**.

Example: — Чем это так пахнет? — У меня **молоко убежало**!

Meaning: — What's that smell? — My milk **boiled over**!

15. **Начистить репу какому-либо перцу** [na-chI-stit' rE-pu ka-kO-mu ni-bUd' pEr-cu]

I want to say sorry guys, in advance, because the Russian language is so.... I can't even find the right word for it!

But let me explain.

The direct translation of this phrase is **"peel the turnip of some pepper"**. It makes no sense, I know. Let me break it down, and explain what each word means. Here we have **"a turnip"** which here means **"head"**. Next, we have **"to peel"** which means **"to fight", "to hit"** and finally, **"some pepper"** means **"some guy"**. If you put it together, you'll find out that it means **" to hit the head of some guy"**.

Turnip, pepper, to peel... Uhhh, the whole garden!!

Example: — Давай **начистим репу этому перцу**! — Без проблем!

Meaning: — Let's **beat this guy up**! — No problem!

16. **Тянуть кота за хвост** [tya-nUt' ka-tA za hvost]

Here's another funny phrase that is translated as **"pull the cat by the tail"**.

Don't feel sorry for the cat! There is no harming of animals involved! It is just a phrase which means **"to postpone for a long time"**, **"to delay"**, **"to procrastinate"**.

Example: — Ты сделала свой проект? — Еще нет. — Хватит **тянуть кота за хвост**!

Meaning: — Have you done your project? — Not yet. — Stop **procrastinating**!

Also, there is a second version of the phrase which is even funnier, but less acceptable, so make sure you say it among your close friends. You can pull a cat not only by the tail, but by the balls! Haha!

Another example: Не **тяни кота за яйца**! Скажи Елене, что любишь ее!

Meaning: **Don't delay**! Tell Elena that you love her!

17. **Море по колено** [mO-re pa ka-lE-na]

The translation of this phrase is **"the sea is knee-deep"**. The Russians use it when they want to say that they are not afraid of anything, or when they describe someone who is reckless.

Example: — Он что вообще ничего не боится? — Да, ему **море по колено**.

Meaning: — Is he not afraid of anything at all? — Yeah, he **is not afraid**.

18. **Наломать дров** [na-la-mAt' drof]

We can translate this phrase as **"to break the firewood"**.

This means making stupid mistakes, making a number of ill-conceived actions, as a result of which you will have to redo the work again.

Example: — Я с ним разберусь! — Будь осторожен и не **наломай дров**!

Meaning: — I'm gonna fight with him! — Be careful and don't **make stupid mistakes**!

19. **Накраситься как матрешка** [na-krA-sit-sya kak ma-tryO-shka]

I love this phrase and find it very funny. It means **"to put on makeup like a matryoshka"**.

I guess you all know what a matryoshka is?

The Russians say it when someone wears very bright make up, like a matryoshka has.

Example: — Почему ты расстался с Аней? — Она **красится как матрешка** каждый день.

Meaning: — Why did you break up with Ann? —She **wears make up like a matryoshka** every day.

So, my dear Russia-lovers, these were the top 20 most confusing Russian phrases for your information, but this is not the end.

CHAPTER 11

Russian humor and jokes

I want to show you guys some funny jokes about Russia and Russian people.

You might not be able to fully understand all of them, but I hope you will find them funny anyway!

P.S. These jokes are not written by me, they are very old and I just want to share them with you guys.

1. I was drinking alcohol with Russians for a whole night. They were trying to convince me that Russia is a horrible country with awful roads, and when I finally agreed with them, they hit me in face.

2. An Italian man was trying to sign up at the gym in Russia. The woman behind the desk asked him for his otchestvo, or patronymic, which is like a middle name taken from your father's name. He told her he didn't have one, so she looked at him pitifully and said, 'Oh, you poor thing!'

3. — I met my wife at a disco...

— Wow! How romantic!

— Sure, it can't be more romantic! I thought she was sitting at home with the children!

4. A man and a woman are having breakfast. The man says

— Prepare me a toast with butter and caviar.

The woman carefully spreads butter and caviar on a piece of bread and hands it to him. He eats it and a couple of minutes later asks again:

—— Please make me another one!

This time she replies:

—— No, sorry. This was just the demo of a caring woman. Should you want to unlock the full licensed version you will need to register for marriage.

5. — Why do the Russians drink vodka so much?

— To at least for a moment forget that they live in the best country.

6. — Why don't Russians celebrate Halloween?

— Because it sucks to take your coat off every time you want to get candy.

7. The Americans created a machine which translates from Russian into English. The machine first smoked, and then exploded after hearing Russian speech.

8. A Russian, an American and a German where arguing about whose echo would last longer. They went to the mountains. The German shouted and his echo lasted 5 seconds. The American shouted and his echo lasted 30 seconds .The Russian man came out and shouted,

"Guys, there is vodka for free!!!" and then said "Where? !!!!!!" — his echo was there for an hour.

8. We are Russians, we can break any laws, except one ... Do not put an empty bottle on the table!

9. An American says to a Russian "I can imagine how you dine: an oak table, on the table: a bottle of vodka, brown bread, herring, onions, porridge, dumplings. Under the table is a gun. On the wall there is a balalaika and a budenovka. There is a tank in the courtyard, and a bear on the porch."

The Russian responds: "What the hell?! Why only one bottle of vodka?!"

10. To have a good memory, it must be trained, by memorizing texts, for example. To have strong muscles, they must be trained, by lifting weights, for example. The Russian man wants to have a trained liver.

So my friends, these were some funny or maybe not so funny jokes about Russia. They are old and have lots of stereotypes but still...

On this beautiful note guys, I need to finish this book about Russian slang and curse words. I hope you enjoyed it and found some information that was useful to you.

I tried hard to select the most used and most popular words and phrases. Of course, I know it's hard for you to understand many of them. In order to truly understand Russian language, you must understand the Russian soul. People used to say that Russians have a very deep, poetic soul, so it's no wonder why there are so many Russian authors and poets that write about love, life and soul. They have the most popular works in the world. I bet everybody in the world knows Dostoevsky, Tolstoy, Mayakovsky, Yesenin etc. Russian people may seem too brutal with their appearance, behavior and language, including slang and curse language. But in reality, we are the most hospitable, kindest and funniest people on Earth. We like deep conversations and old music, and we are always happy to see you if you want to come over.

So if YOU are a FAN of Russia, or you just want to travel to the Russian Federation, you are always welcome! Don't be afraid and if you have doubts, Russia will melt your heart with its huge beauty, cute girls, delicious food, amazing nature, snowy landscapes in winter, and green ones in summer. Don't believe all those silly stereotypes. Most of them are old and they still exists in our jokes just to have a good laugh. In the reality, Russia is not like in those myths from the Internet. Learn Russian language, don't be afraid of difficulties and don't forget to read this book over again if you plan to visit our huge country. I promise, it will help you to make lot's of Russian friends!

I am sure you will fall in love with our big beautiful country. Bye for now! Russia is already waiting for you <3.